An Illuminating Experience

About the author

Born in the Merseyside area, Gordon Medlicott served in the Merchant Navy before joining the Trinity House Lighthouse Service in 1966.

Travelling extensively around the coasts of England, Wales and the Channel Islands, he completed 32 years of service, visiting 22 lighthouses and one Lighthouse Control Centre. During the latter years of his service major refurbishment and the automation of the Lighthouse Service was in progress, producing a more streamlined and economical, but demanned service. Gordon was eventually forced into early retirement in 1998.

An Illuminating Experience

Gordon Medlicott

Best Wishes
Gordon Medlicott

Whittles Publishing

Published by
Whittles Publishing,
Dunbeath,
Caithness KW6 6EY,
Scotland, UK

www.whittlespublishing.com

© 2009 G Medlicott

ISBN 978-1904445-64-7

Cover photograph of Longstone Light courtesy of Chris Nicholson.

Printed by Bell & Bain Ltd., Glasgow

To my wife Louise, and daughters Paula and Anne, who without complaint made my 32 years in the lighthouse service possible.

Also for the many lighthouse keepers who have become part of our maritime history, and contributed to a service dedicated to the safe passage of mariners and travellers.

CONTENTS

Acknowledgements

The author and publisher gratefully acknowledge the following for permission to reproduce their copyright materials: HRH The Duke of Edinburgh for the full transcript of this speech given at North Foreland lighthouse in November 1998 (p. 104); Trinity House for the Keepers' pay scale 1968 (p. 121); Louise Medlicott and the Association of Lighthouse Keepers for extracts of her article in *Lamp*, March 1994 (p. 38)

The author would also like to thank all those who kindly provided images and assisted in the publication of this book.

Preface

The following is an autobiographical account of my time in the Trinity House Lighthouse Service from day one, and covers a period when the Service went from oil lights to satellites, from clockwork to computers, and communications evolved from semaphore to mobile phones, and so on until the final farewell … an interesting experience!

I joined the Trinity House Lighthouse Service in July 1966 as a Supernumerary Keeper tending oil lights rotated by a hand-wound clockwork mechanism and handling explosive fog signals. Little did I realise that I would witness, and become part of, a new industrial revolution created by the microchip that would cause a new technological age to sweep through this archaic industry. This technology meant that I would see lighthouses unmanned, operated by remote control via telemetry links to a computer, and I would have the capability to receive and transmit information provided by satellites as part of a Global Positioning System.

Gordon Medlicott

Editor's note

For the internal consistency of an account that spans the metrication of Trinity House, feet, yards, miles and other imperial units of measurement have been used throughout. The notable exceptions are the references for the Global Positioning System, which did not come into use until the later stages of this account, where distances are expressed in metres.

INTRODUCTION

As an island nation Britain depends heavily on imports and exports. Look in your shopping basket and see the number of countries from around the world where many of these items come from. As part of this commercial enterprise lighthouse keepers played a vital role: they maintained the navigation lights for the safety not only of these cargoes, but also of the men and women who man our ships. Lighthouse keepers were also the unpaid eyes for HM Coastguard, HM Customs & Excise, and the rescue services such as the RNLI, and RAF rescue helicopters. Many universities and organisations such as the RSPB and Greenpeace also asked keepers to contribute their time in recording particular kinds of data from their isolated positions. The Meteorological Office paid keepers a nominal fee to record weather data on an hourly basis to enable them to collate and broadcast a national weather forecast. Listen to the shipping forecast today and you will hear that these reports are now from 'automatic weather stations'. Commercial advertisers have also used the image of the lighthouse to sell products, capitalising on the lighthouse's traditional depiction as a symbol of strength, security and reliability.

Lighthouses have also through the years been used as a platform to test various kinds of equipment and new inventions. Marconi experimented with sound transmissions between the East Goodwin Lightship and South Foreland Lighthouse, while Augustin Fresnel developed the prismatic dioptric lens (the theory of which is still used in car headlights today). Aimé Argand designed the smokeless oil lamp, and Faraday and Holmes installed magneto-electric machines in lighthouses to test the feasibility of a continuous electric light.

A new industrial revolution

During the 1970s and 1980s I was to experience a period of great change within the lighthouse service: until then the age-old, tried and tested methods of operating and living at a lighthouse had been maintained at certain stations. Change within the Service tended to take a long time, but this period saw an unprecedented explosion of activity that within just two decades led to the complete automation of all our lighthouses. During that time many of the older keepers, myself included, scoffed at the suggestion that the lighthouses standing many miles out at sea would or could be operated without the presence of a keeper ... but lo and behold, here we are today, nostalgically reminiscing about our time in the Service and the way it used to be!

Before joining the lighthouse service I had given little thought to what the living conditions aboard a lighthouse would be like. With a Merchant Navy background I probably subconsciously thought they would be similar to those onboard a ship. The comfortable accommodation I encountered at my first shore-based station didn't prompt me to have any further thoughts on the subject, but I would quickly learn that living conditions between the various stations differed tremendously. Some of the offshore stations, with no bathroom or electricity available, were, to say the least, pretty basic. The large amounts of fuel consumed and the limited ventilation meant that condensation was not only prevalent, it was a constant companion.

Modernisation and automation of lighthouses began with the shore-based stations where access was freely and readily available. Then came the turn of the island stations, where it was always going to be a more difficult and time-consuming task, and perhaps at times a frustrating one owing to adverse weather conditions. However, it was the tower rock stations that were, in logistical terms, to be the most difficult, not only because of their remote locations but because any materials required had to be packaged into manageable sizes as everything had to be transferred from a small boat to the lighthouse by hand.

It was the development and installation of the rooftop helipad, and the introduction of helicopters in general that brought about the rapid change, since many of the traditional problems of transporting goods aboard ships and boats were eliminated, as was the necessary, and often frustrating, wait for reasonable sea and weather conditions.

Advance storage of equipment onboard a station was always a problem, owing to lack of space, as was accommodation for engineers or contractors who had to be on site. Many of these visiting personnel found they had to sleep on the floor of what was to become an overcrowded living space, and having to arrange with and teach outsiders how to live and integrate with the permanent staff of keepers was not always a harmonious experience.

Throughout the period that contractors and engineers were aboard these lighthouses fixing and establishing new systems, it was down to the keepers to maintain their own usual routines and service requirements for the safety of mariners, as well as maintaining the cleanliness of the buildings and continuity of domestic services. Some visiting contractors appreciated the dilemma of the keepers who had to continue watches throughout the night and would therefore have to sleep during the day, but others were so self-centred and oblivious to the needs of others that they simply continued to carry on their work as if they were on a normal building site, which at times led to the occasional frayed temper and confrontation. On one or two occasions it was necessary for me as Principal Keeper of a station to say to the heads of our engineering departments that enough was enough, and that on the grounds of safety and well-being of my own crew, I would only accept a limited number of extra men at a time to live with us on the lighthouse, which I'm afraid, didn't always go down too well. It was all well and good heads of departments saying they had a job and a deadline to meet, but it was we the keepers who had to put up with the disruption and the cramped living conditions, as well as having the increased workload of keeping the buildings habitable through the dust and dirt generated, and handling extra helicopters and boats to keep the station stocked with essential domestic supplies.

I

Entering the Lighthouse Service

My background before entering the Lighthouse Service is that as a young man I served in the Merchant Navy for approximately six years; then my marriage in 1963 to Louise took me to a small town in central Lancashire where I took a shore job. However, within two years, with redundancy looming and little prospect of further work in the town, I proposed returning to sea. The standard contract of engagement for seamen signing on on foreign-going vessels at that time was for two years, with the option on return of a discharge at the first UK port when a man could leave a vessel if he so wished, but in reality few ships were ever away for that period of time. Accrued paid shore leave, taken on return to the UK, was calculated on the basis of one day for each Sunday actually spent steaming at sea (in excess of eight hours), plus one day for each completed month of the voyage, so it wasn't over generous, and with the uncertainty about how long I would be away from home at any one time, it wasn't an ideal situation for a young married man. Not wishing to leave the sea, I felt a compromise would be employment with Trinity House, the Lighthouse Service for England, Wales, the Channel Islands and Gibraltar because once you were established it gave far greater leave periods than the Merchant Navy: after 56 days at a lighthouse (on a regular fixed-date basis) I was guaranteed 28 days ashore, so I would know exactly when I was coming and going, and the work had the benefit of being 'at sea' to boot. An added bonus, which at that time seemed rather attractive, was that after promotion to Assistant Keeper either accommodation would be provided or an allowance paid in lieu, so the prospect of joining Trinity House seemed to be a better deal.

This idyllic lifestyle I was now dreaming of did, however, have a drawback: it would only come about after I was trained and had been appointed to the rank of

Assistant Keeper. Training was deemed to be for *up to* five years, with promotion being made in order of seniority as and when a vacancy occurred or on completion of five years' service, whichever was the sooner, so there was some uncertainty as to just how long one would take to become established. However, it was necessary to secure employment with the Service in the first place.

Trinity House, London (Courtesy Trinity House Collection)

TRINITY HOUSE – THE CORPORATION

The Corporation of Trinity House describes itself as 'a unique maritime organisation which throughout its history has had as its prime objective the safety of shipping and the welfare of seafarers'.
It presents its three main roles as:

- the general lighthouse authority for England, Wales and the Channel Islands and Gibraltar, providing aids to general navigation – lighthouses, light vessels, buoys, beacons and radio navigation systems;
- a charitable organisation for the safety, welfare and training of mariners and the relief of those who are in financial distress;
- a deep-sea pilotage authority.

What had been a fraternity of mariners of a semi-religious, charitable character was granted a Royal Charter by Henry VIII in 1514, under the name of Guild of the Holy Trinity, with general powers to regulate pilotage. Its link to lighthouses originates in the Act of Parliament of 1566 giving it powers to set up 'so many beacons, marks and signs for the sea ... whereby the dangers must be avoided and escaped and ships the better to come unto their ports without peril.' The first lighthouse built by Trinity House was at Lowestoft in 1609. In 1836 lighthouses in private ownership were compulsorily purchased and placed under the management of Trinity House. Now the only lighthouse operated outside Trinity House is at Happisburgh, Norfolk, and is maintained by a trust.

TRINITY HOUSE – THE BUILDINGS

When the Corporation of Trinity House was first formed in 1514 it began at Deptford. It later moved to Ratcliffe, and then around 1618 moved again to Stepney. In 1660 a relocation to Water Lane ended in 1666 with the Great Fire of London. Rebuilt in 1667 the new building only lasted 47 years before it, too, was burned down. In 1793 Samuel Wyatt designed the present building now occupied at Tower Hill, London. Constructed of Portland Stone with Doric columns and pilasters, the exterior of the façade is adorned with cherubs holding anchors, compasses and marine charts. On the night of 27 December 1940 the building received a direct hit from an incendiary bomb which destroyed most of the interior, along with the historical records and treasures of the Corporation. When the war was over Sir Albert Richardson, architect for the Corporation, restored the burnt-out building to its former glory. The work was completed in 1953 and officially reopened by Her Majesty Queen Elizabeth II.

I presented myself for interview at Trinity House on Tower Hill, London, where I learned that as a lighthouse keeper I was expected to supply my own food, and live within the depot area to which I was assigned, otherwise I would have to pay my own travelling expenses between my home and any lighthouse to which I was sent. As this was not something I had had to do in the Merchant Navy, I had second thoughts. It was some months later, that, with work at home becoming increasingly short, I reapplied for a second interview, which to my surprise was granted. Following an entrance examination and medical check I was interviewed by the Chief Superintendent, Captain Thompson, who, after flattering me on my seamanship credentials and sea experience, attempted to persuade me to sign on for the Lightvessel Service instead of the Lighthouse Service … 'fear not' … he then told me that I would have a job for life!

After signing the Official Secrets Act it was a case of signing on the dotted line and then waiting for a date to join the training school.

Bread and oil

The date for me to attend the school finally came through in July, and on the 18th I travelled by train to Harwich, where I was to spend the next four weeks. Situated in a single room at the back of the Trinity House Depot building, the school was run by a Principal Keeper named Frank Moore. As there was only one other entrant at the school, Fred Rosewall, we shared digs in town, which was only a five-minute walk away.

Instruction in the operation and maintenance of an incandescent oil burner or IOB (paraffin lamp – see Appendix 4) took me by surprise as I hadn't considered

Harwich Depot in which the training school was located (Courtesy Simon Beesley)

that our lighthouses were still operated by oil, and to maintain them it was necessary to learn the skills of soldering and repairing copper fuel pipes. Other required skills were the art of cooking and breadmaking along with signalling (Morse code and semaphore), rope and knot work. No instruction of any kind was given in the maintenance or care of either lighting plant or compressors or, more importantly, in the safe handling of explosives used for fog signals. Having benefited from a sound basic training at sea, which had stood me in good stead for the job I did there, I felt the overall instruction here didn't really give a sense of what would be expected of us when we joined a lighthouse. However, at the end of the fourth week, armed with certificates of competence (!) and kitted out in uniform, complete with brass buttons and white peaked cap, I left the school as a Supernumerary Assistant Keeper (SAK). I was now on the threshold of a new career but, given that I wasn't required to report to my first lighthouse until the following Monday, I was free to go home for the weekend.

LIGHTHOUSE PATENTS

Even after the incorporation of Trinity House by Royal Charter, and much to their annoyance, the Crown felt itself to be above the Guild's regulations and continued to sell much-sought-after patents to speculators and court hangers-on, allowing them to build lighthouses, having no scruples about collecting an annual monetary return for the privilege.

New horizons

I had been assigned to the Swansea Depot, which looked after the lights of the Bristol Channel and Welsh coast, and it was to the stations of this area that I would in due course be sent to obtain certificates of proficiency in the different types of equipment used, such as optics, clockwork drives, electric light equipment, fog signal equipment and radio beacons. This was something I looked forward to.

Leaving home on the Monday I travelled by train to North Devon via Manchester, Bristol, Exeter and Barnstaple, then by local bus to the village of Hartland. It was from here that I took a taxi for the final five miles along narrow single-track country lanes in the company of an elderly driver named Mr Huggins to Hartland Point Lighthouse.

Situated at the south-western end of the Bristol Channel, the lighthouse is dramatically perched some 400 feet below a cliff on the plateau of a small isthmus at the point of a headland, and is approached from an extremely steep and winding roadway with views out to Lundy Island.

Hartland Point

Enclosed within a boundary wall, this is a shore-based station with three resident keepers and their families living in their own quarters within the single main building. I was billeted on my own in a fairly comfortable two-roomed bedsit on the first floor, the access to which was from the spiral stairway halfway up the lighthouse tower. Overawed by the wonderment of actually being on a lighthouse and by the beauty of its location, I spent some time investigating my new temporary home and meeting my colleagues, who were Peter Edwards PK, Ivor Pritchard, senior AK and Ron Churchill AK.

I was placed in a watch with the senior keeper to be instructed in watchkeeping, the use of the fog signal engines, and the maintenance of the light and lens equipment, along with other mysterious and traditional ways of the Lighthouse Service. Looking around the station I could see that the brasswork on the window fasteners, handrails and door handles gleamed and the windows sparkled, in fact the whole working area of the station was unbelievably clean, even the engine-room floor shone with red polish, so it looked more like a spanking new museum. In the lantern there was a beautiful double-tiered optical lens that must have been six feet in diameter and over ten feet tall that rotated by floating in a bath of mercury, inside each section of which was a 3,000-watt lamp the size of a football, the largest electric light bulb I had ever seen, and like a glittering jewel it was absolutely magical. The engine room housed a standby diesel-powered generator to maintain the light in the event of a mains power failure, a mains-powered rotary air compressor, along with its diesel-driven standby, and three huge air receivers and electrical cabinets for the operation and control of the diaphone fog signal.

Bi-form lens

MERCURY FLOAT TURNTABLES

This type of rotation was first devised by a Mr O. Bourdelles. Late in the 19th century the design of turntables had progressed to the point where it became possible to turn massive lens arrays, weighing many tons, with the pressure applied through a little finger. Previous arrays had revolved on a turntable supported by rollers on a circular track. This entailed high friction forces and required considerable power to rotate them; heavy wear on components led to unreliable rotation speeds and the weights on the clockwork mechanisms were increasingly heavy and thus laborious to wind from the bottom to the top of the tower. James Chance, realising that the mercury trough would greatly reduce friction and wear on the existing roller bearings, incorporated it into his turntables with great success.

ELECTRIC LIGHT

On average a filament lamp gives ten times the light of that of a vaporised burner (IOB).

The routine watch system of split day and night shifts was very similar to that used in the Merchant Navy so I was familiar with it, and apart from having to live on my own, I settled in OK. It did not at this point seem odd, nor did it cross my mind that I would ever find it to be otherwise, that I should have a bathroom, toilet, running water, central heating, or electric light, and I enjoyed the luxury of all these without question.

The keepers' responsibility when on duty was to ensure that the light was exhibited throughout the hours of darkness, and that the fog signal was operated as and when required. It was *not*, contrary to belief, to watch for or to communicate with shipping. As the watchkeeping position here was in a windowless room at the base of the tower an electronic control panel monitored the light, but a frequent look outside was always necessary to check the rotating beams of light as their width would indicate if there was a presence of fog. Every four hours the duty watchman filled in two logbooks, noting local weather conditions and anything else of interest, all entries being made with a nib pen and ink, one of these books being sent to the District Depot as a monthly return, the other retained on station as an annual record. In the event of a ship declaring weather conditions as the cause of an incident then the records at the lighthouse could be seconded as evidence for or against.

I was also introduced to the 'book of regulations', the written law stating what lighthouse keepers could or could not do, many of the regulations being archaic and pointless in this day and age. It was noted, however, that 'under no pretext should a man leave his watch position', and that only a straight-backed chair would be provided, to prevent him falling asleep, and that falling asleep on duty was a sackable offence. When off duty I was able to wander along the clifftop paths, visit the local Coastguard Station situated directly above the lighthouse, or walk into Hartland to the village shops five miles away, read, or just listen to the radio (it would be some years before Trinity House got round to issuing televisions to lighthouses). What I didn't know was that over the next 12 months I would be required to travel at short notice to various stations within the area to cover for sickness, etc., so it was with some surprise that after only a week or so at Hartland I learned that I was to relieve one of the keepers granted compassionate leave at Bull Point Lighthouse near Woolacombe.

The nearest village to Bull Point was Mortehoe, a sleepy little place reached after a leisurely journey by local train from Bideford, stopping at quaint little country stations along the line. The taxi ride from Woolacombe to Mortehoe and the lighthouse across rolling green fields didn't take too long. Arriving in mid afternoon I found the keepers out in the yard looking seaward at a Trinity House tender in the bay with its launch in the water. Apparently a fishing vessel had sunk

Bull Point

right in front of the lighthouse the previous evening and the ship was laying a wreck buoy over its present position to prevent further mishap. Bull Point was another family station, and to my astonishment I found that my accommodation here was a dilapidated little caravan parked in the lighthouse yard; with no bathroom and only a chemical toilet in an outhouse some way away, I was not best pleased.

My colleagues here were Bill Mortimer PK and Roy Howes AK; the man I had come to relieve was the assistant keeper Kevin Wood.

The station was built in 1879 with a short tower standing in front of a row of three cottages and, seaward of the tower, the engine room housing a standby diesel generator, two huge water-cooled engines and three air receivers for use with the fog signal. The foghorns were rectangular and approximately seven feet high; one was attached to the front exterior wall of the engine room, a second to the side, and very impressive they were too. The light at Bull Point was powered from the mains electricity with a 1,000-watt lamp. Mounted on a central pedestal, the lens was not as large or as impressive as that at Hartland, but still a beautiful thing in its own right, and the station was equally clean and bright. I was somewhat surprised to find that, despite the advent of ship-to-shore radio, the keepers here were still required to hoist a black canvas cone on a flag mast to warn coastal shipping of an impending storm: an upward-pointing cone denoted a northerly gale, and a downward pointing one, a southerly gale. This system had been used quite effectively long before the days of radio communication, but nowadays had to be considered quite primitive.

I was put into the watch routine under the same conditions as the other keepers and enjoyed the peacefulness of my first night watches on my own, and over the following days I took advantage of walking around some of this beautiful area when off duty. On being relieved at Bull Point I was pleased to learn that I was to return to Hartland and I enjoyed the return journey. However, my contentment was cut short: within a few days I was required to travel to Flatholm Island because one of the keepers there had been taken ill. As this was to be my first offshore station I didn't quite know what to expect. I travelled by various buses

Small lens at Bull Point

and trains to arrive late in the evening at Barry Island in South Wales, from where I would depart by boat the following morning. After reporting to the local agent I had to find digs and a food shop where I could buy supplies.

Leaving Barry Harbour the next morning at about 7.30 a.m. in a small boat it took me approximately 30 minutes to cross the tide-ripped waters of the channel to reach the island where I was greeted by my two new fellow keepers: the senior keeper Eddie Bell AK, and Dave Erickson AK.

Napoleonic defences

Flatholm, set between Cardiff and Weston-super-Mare in the Bristol Channel, is an island of approximately 80 acres that was once farmed. The farmhouse, although unoccupied at the time of my visit, was still used as an occasional weekend retreat. In Napoleonic times the island had been fortified, and the cannon were still in position in their stone-built circular gun emplacements, with barrack buildings, ammunition storerooms and an isolation hospital. Of course all were now derelict, but gave some idea of the important role the island had played in the defence of this area.

The keepers' flat-roofed living quarters, isolated from the lighthouse tower, stand close to the engine room and consist of a square single-storey building with three bedrooms, a kitchen and a living room. There was no bathroom. There was, however, a full-sized bath in one corner of the kitchen, but no drainage pipes, nor water on tap, and the only water available in the kitchen was supplied from an underground storage tank by means of a hand-operated rotary pump above the sink; hot water was supplied from a large iron kettle kept on the top of the coal range. After settling in I was given the 'grand tour', and the first thing that struck me was how bare everything was … bare walls … windows … shelves and

Flatholm Island

floors, that bareness being reflected by the highly polished linoleum on the floor and the overall cleanliness of the place. Painted in a uniform manner, the top half of the walls was cream, divided by a thin black line from the buff lower half, with the skirtings a dark stone colour. The only decoration adorning the interior walls was official instructions on how to operate a particular item of equipment. I later heard an ex-serviceman use the expression 'as bare as a barrack room', which I think just about summed it up. The bedrooms proved to be equally bare, without curtains or rugs, just the dark brown linoleum floor, a steel-framed bed, and a free-standing chest of drawers.

Lighting in the living room and kitchen was from a pressure oil lamp (Tilley lamp), and a small hand-held wick lamp was used in the bedroom. With no heating except the kitchen range and a coal fire in the living room, the quarters were not the warmest place in the world. Only a chemical toilet was available in an outhouse, and with no bathroom a wash-down at the kitchen sink in front of the coal-fired stove was the order of the day, so life was pretty basic here. I was, however, somewhat surprised to find that there was a battery-operated television, which proved to be a gift to the station from a private organisation ashore, and although permission was obtained from Trinity House for it to be here, the donors had also had to supply the batteries and a power pack (for conversion to 240 volt), and agree to maintain it. The concession made by Trinity House was to supply a small charging engine and the fuel to run it. Communication with the shore was via a ship-to-shore radio–telephone, with messages or link calls (telephone) being made through a coast radio station (in this case Mumbles), or via a very poor VHF telephone link, but generally, apart from a daily test, unless it was important or urgent, no messages were sent or received.

The lighthouse tower stands several hundred yards away from the keepers' quarters, around its base are the old family living quarters used many years ago when two families operated the station; these are now used for visiting mechanics and maintenance personnel, etc. The tall open tower with its long spiral staircase carries the lantern with a fixed lens, a clockwork rotating occulting mechanism and a 100-mm IOB lamp. Although I had been trained in the basics of lighting and maintaining an oil light, I was given a quick lesson on how to 'light up' on an actual lighthouse. One of the major points stressed was that tools kept in the vicinity of the lamp for use in an emergency should be kept in the *order of use* and *not* in size order, which, although it looked neater, was totally impractical, because if the light should go out, the lantern room was plunged into complete darkness and, the lamp components being extremely hot, it was important for the keeper to be able to put his hand on the appropriate spanner or pliers instantly, and not have to grope around using the trial and error technique. In this situation, if the keeper was quick enough he could reinstate the light without needing to install the standby lamp or preheat the main fuel vaporiser again. All the

IOB lamp

12

equipment on this station looked as if it belonged to another century, especially the monstrous 22 hp Ruston Hornsby oil engines (*c.*1908 – see Appendix 2) with their 16-inch horizontal cylinder and six-foot high flywheel, the steelwork and brass fittings of which were all polished and gleaming like exhibits in a museum … magnificent.

Trumpets and ghosts

Situated on the roof of the engine room were two of the largest trumpets imaginable – they must have been all of seven feet tall at the mouth – and the noise from them when operating was really mind blowing. Because of the distance between the tower and the fog signal, when both the light and the fog signal were in operation it was a requirement that a second keeper should be in the engine room while the duty keeper was tending the light, but in practice this didn't happen; the duty keeper tended both locations, thereby not having to call out a second man unless he encountered a problem. During my off-duty time I was able to practise starting, stopping and maintaining the engines and learned how they worked, and how the station routine operated, which made life a little easier. Routine played a big part in keepers' lives, and the morning watch routine generally followed a similar pattern in all lighthouses. The duty watchman, commencing in the lantern, put the light out at daybreak, hung the huge lantern

Flatholm's fog horn with tower in distance (Courtesy Chris Foulds)

curtains around the windows (to prevent the sun passing through the lenses and causing a fire) then, after preparing and positioning the spare lamp for lighting up the following evening, polished the massive lens and its equipment and cleaned the windows, by which time the lamp he had removed using pliers and other tools would be cool enough to clean and polish and be prepared for use as the standby that evening. After ensuring there was sufficient oil for the following 24 hours, the duty keeper washed all the floors, not only in the tower, but the living quarters as well. The kitchen and living room were cleaned out, as was the cooking range fire, and the coal buckets replenished. The oil lamps from the quarters were trimmed and refilled, and if the engines had been used overnight for fog then the engine and engine room also had to be cleaned. Between 10 a.m.

GLAZING

Diagonal glazing was introduced in 1849 as it offered the minimum disruption of light in any direction, thereby eliminating the previous illusion of a multiple flashing light as the beam passed vertical bars. It also created a stronger structure by allowing the use of curved braces, seen on the exterior of earlier lanterns, to be discontinued.

and 12 noon each day Monday to Saturday, the morning duty keeper was joined by the off-duty men in keeping the station buildings and grounds spick and span, doing any jobs the PK could think of, so our regular working week consisted of 56 hours' watchkeeping plus any fog time, and the extra two hours daily.

Cooking was done by each man in turn, each being 'cook of the day' every third day, when he was responsible for producing a cooked midday meal. As the only means of preserving food was in a paraffin-operated fridge, fresh food didn't keep too long, so meals were by necessity pretty basic, being prepared from whatever was available and edible, supplemented by tinned products. Some men were excellent cooks while others found it an effort, but as a rule the midday meal was always acceptable and plentiful, and as the men all sat down together it was a time to discuss world affairs and reflect on life in general. Each keeper made his own bread and cakes, with varying degrees of success, and as we had no access to fresh milk we used tins of condensed milk (it would be some time before freeze-dried and UHT milk and other similar foods were available on the market), but generally the men looked after themselves fairly well. During the afternoons, for those of the regular crew who were so inclined, there were always the gardens that surrounded the building in which to grow fresh produce while others indulged in hobbies, of which there were many. My hobby at that time was making children's soft toys.

The final week of a duty period was 'relief clean-up week' when, in addition to the daily cleaning, every room in the lighthouse and living quarters down to its darkest recesses, was turned out, and woe betide any crew that left anything dirty or out of place!

After four weeks at Flatholm I came ashore on the tender *Alert*, (there were at that time five or six lighthouse tenders based at various depots around the coast and used for maintenance of buoys, lightvessels and lighthouses; those I remember are, *Alert*, *Stella*, *Ready*, *Siren*, and the flagship *Patricia*). After *Alert* had completed the relief of the other lighthouses and lightvessels in the Bristol Channel I was landed at Swansea and allowed home on two weeks' leave. I later came to learn that compared to other stations where they had electricity and more modern amenities Flatholm, because of its very basic and sparse conditions, was considered by some to be an unofficial punishment station, but despite this I enjoyed my time there and found the island interesting and the peaceful surroundings enjoyable.

Many stories are told about strange and mysterious happenings aboard lighthouses, and at Flatholm it was of the ghost of the 'White Lady' that inhabited the tower. When entering the tower the keeper picked up from the floor a small oil lamp and, holding it about chest height, approached a glazed inner door that would admit him to the tower stairway. It was at this point that many keepers had reported seeing a fleeting glimpse of the White Lady, but on one occasion the keeper was so frightened that without thought he threw the lighted lamp at the apparition and fled. The burning oil from the lamp set fire to the wooden interior door causing some concern for the safety of the tower. I am sure that when submitted, the official report failed to mention that the poor frightened keeper had been primed by his colleagues about the ghost before he went to the tower, or that what he actually saw was probably his own reflection in the glass panel.

LIGHTHOUSE MEMORIAL WINDOWS

Bristol Cathedral has a lighthouse memorial window to George Robinson, Inspector of Works to Trinity House, who drowned while crossing from Flatholm Island in the Bristol Channel.

My return to duty saw me yet again travelling to Hartland Point as a relief keeper to allow each of the regular crew members there to take their four weeks annual leave, so I was to be there for three months. Because of this extended period I asked the Principal Keeper if my wife and baby daughter could stay with me at the station for the duration, for which permission was granted by the Superintendent. However, after approximately four weeks a second SAK arrived on station, and as he would share the quarters with me, my wife and daughter had to leave and return home, but at least we had been able to spend a little extra time together.

With the arrival of the second SAK, I found that as the more experienced of the two it was I who was instructed to report to the district depot at Swansea where I was to join a regular major relief of the Bristol Channel lights, and transfer to the North Light at Lundy Island.

RELIEFS

Each lighthouse was manned by three keepers. On a major relief two keepers (one being the Principal Keeper) relieved two of the three men onboard. The remaining third man would be relieved halfway through that duty period on a minor relief at what was then the completion of his duty period. So, although the men were on the lighthouse for two months, a relief took place every month.

The relief procedure was much the same wherever I went throughout the country, with keepers following more or less the same routine. Immediately after the changeover, from either a boat or helicopter, all the relief gear from the landing or helipad would be stowed away and radio communication with the boat or helicopter concerned would be stood down.

The incoming crew would unpack foodstuffs into appropriate store cupboards, bridges, freezers, etc., then newspapers and magazine would be produced, and over tea in the kitchen we talked of what had been happening since we had all last met a month before. We would then unpack and stow the rest of the gear, make up the bed, and change into working rig; the uniform would not see the light of day again until the next relief.

After the incoming crew had settled in, the watch system would be sorted out, each man discovering what duty he was on, as in many cases the remaining keeper would have filled in the watch duty while the relief was taking place. The PK might do a tour of the station to check equipment, read log and repair books, stock lists, etc., to acquire a full picture of the current stock position of fuel and water, and of what had been happening whilst he had been on leave.

Then it was business as usual ...

2

Cruising the Bristol Channel

After obtaining my supplies and storing them aboard the ship I met my other colleague for the North Light along with those for the relief of Flatholm and South Lundy lights, and the crews for Scarweather, Breaksea, Helwick, St Gowan and English & Welsh Grounds Lightvessels. After sailing to each destination it was interesting to see the procedure as the lightvessels were re-fuelled and watered, and the men replaced. Arriving off the north end of Lundy Island it was necessary to transfer from the ship to a motor launch, when the

North Light at Lundy (Courtesy Chris Foulds)

dangers of trying to board a small craft that was swiftly rising and falling and crashing against the ship's side became a serious worry. It was equally dangerous after we had been ferried to a small stone set off directly below the lighthouse, where it was almost impossible, because of the heavy sea swell, to stand upright while trying to get ashore without injury. With the job finally done and the keepers safely exchanged, it was then necessary to negotiate a series of steep winding steps set into the cliffside to reach the station. Fortunately our heavy supplies and station stores had been hoisted from the boat in a cargo net and deposited at the top of the cliff long before we arrived there. My colleagues at the north light were Fred Jones PK, and Ted Townsend AK.

North Lundy was, even on the brightest of days, a dark lighthouse: it was situated below the rim of the island and faced north, therefore it never saw the sun. It was also another oil-operated station, its light being operated in the same way as Flatholm but with a 75-mm IOB lamp. The short dumpy tower stood between the dwelling and the engine room, all of which were in a small yard surrounded by a white boundary wall. The lens here was a monstrous thing (I believe it was of French manufacture and weighed four tons); oval shaped, it had two closely set bull's eyes on each side and floated in a trough of mercury to give a double flashing light. Its rotation was from a weight-driven clock. The fog signal differed in that it was a siren operated by a three-cylinder Gardner T3 oil engine that required all three cylinders to be pre-heated with blowlamps before they were started, a different kettle of fish altogether from the big Hornsbys at Flatholm. The keepers' facilities were again sparse, to say the least: no bathroom, no running water and no electric light, but here, too, there was a battery-powered television. One extra piece of equipment I had not encountered before was a radio beacon for which, after a month here, I would receive my certificate of proficiency. A test transmission twice a day, morning and afternoon, was made by radio-telephone with each of the stations in the Bristol Channel 'group', on the completion of which those who were interested would stay 'on air' and pass on service information or gossip.

Lying across the mouth of the Bristol Channel, the island rises 400 feet out of the sea and is three miles long by half a mile wide, with tall forbidding cliffs that make landing difficult, except at one safe beach on the south-eastern side. The island's position was originally marked by a magnificent single lighthouse situated on the highest point, but unfortunately this was obscured by cloud and fog far too frequently, so it was replaced by the two lighthouses we have today, one at each end. The island has had a chequered history, including as a haunt of pirates, but in more settled times has supported a small community of fishermen and farmers, when the flat fertile top at the southern end was used for agriculture. Today the quietness of the island makes it a haven of peace away

RADIO BEACONS

Aids to navigation come in various forms, from unlit daymarks to very sophisticated custom-built lighthouses and fog signals, but radio signals also play a part in navigation, and at certain selected lighthouses Radio Beacons are operated. The method of direction-finding using a radio beacon is a relatively simple one. A vessel can establish an approximate position from a non-directional radio beacon, which is very useful in poor visibility or when navigating out of sight of land. The effective range of this system is limited, with few beacons giving bearings of reasonable accuracy at more than 50 miles. A common arrangement is for six beacons to share one frequency in a six minute cycle, their transmissions being arranged in a strict time schedule so that they do not overlap. In all cases the cycle of the group starts on the hour; thus the first beacon transmits on the hour and subsequently at 06–12–18–24 etc. minutes past. The beacon which is number six will transmit at 05–11–17–23 etc. minutes past the hour. Each station is identified by its call sign in Morse code.

Receiving apparatus onboard a vessel will give a compass bearing along the strongest line of the signal, and several bearings will give a triangulation and position.

from the hustle and bustle and rapid pace of life. Its main concessions are having its own postal service and postage stamps, valued in Puffins (the island once had its own currency called the Puffin).

Lundy Island at this time was privately owned by the Harman family, who kept a summer residence there. A small community of approximately fifteen people live and work here, farming and tourism as their main occupations. Supplies and visitors are brought in by ship from Ilfracombe on a regular basis or as weather permits, and there is a hotel, and various other properties are available for rent during the summer months.

The Lundy puffin stamp

When going to an offshore lighthouse on a regular relief I had to report to the Trinity House Depot at Swansea Docks to join one of the lighthouse tenders, usually the *Alert*, which took out the combined relief crews for the five lightvessels and three lighthouses of the Bristol Channel in one trip. This could sometimes take a day or two to complete, depending on weather conditions. Duty at either

Flatholm or the Lundy lights was, in my case as an SAK, usually for a period of four weeks, but occasionally I was required to do the double turn of eight weeks, for which I was then allowed four weeks' shore leave.

Lawrence Jaeger was the District Clerk for Swansea Depot and dealt with all matters relating to lighthouses and their keepers, ensuring that each station was fully manned, and that SAKs were deployed as necessary to obtain their certificates. He was a man well respected by the keepers, and had always been extremely good and understanding to me during my training period. In my opinion he was the only person at that time within the organisation who understood the problems associated with the job and its effect on families. He always attempted to get the SAKs home for Christmas if possible. For my first Christmas in the Service I was pleased to be at home.

Travelling between stations was to become a regular occurrence during my time as a Supernumerary Keeper; apart from being wherever I was for training, I was also readily available for relief duty anywhere in the district in case of an emergency. Because the period of time I was to spend on duty at a particular lighthouse was always liable to change, the leave periods were equally uncertain, which was all very unsettling for my family.

I made a return to Flatholm early in 1967 for what was known as 'winter duty': it was usual to send a fourth hand there in January and February just to operate the fog signal engines because of the prevalence of fog during these months. The regular duty keeper was stationed at the tower on the other side of the island tending the light and was not supposed to spend any extended time at the engine room but, as described above, the usual practice was in fact for one keeper to do both jobs. Integrating me into the watch routine as a fourth hand meant fewer night watches and other routine duties for each man. As the station had its complement of regular keepers, Colin Nicholls PK, Eddie Bell AK, and Bob Kett AK, the three bedrooms in the main accommodation block were occupied, therefore the only room available for me was at the mechanics' quarters over at the tower. Despite being away from the living quarters I was still very much a part of the crew, and as such took my turn as 'cook of the day' with the other men as well as all the other station activities. With the winter darkness falling by mid-afternoon, it was policy to leave lighting the living-quarter lamps until as late as possible, thereby reducing the need to trim them or replenish their fuel during the night, which was a messy business.

As part of my uniform issue I had what was known as a 'great coat', a full-length double-breasted overcoat with fitted top and extra large collar, and from the waist down a full skirt to the ankle. Around the back at waist level was a double thickness half-belt with six brass buttons, and down the front was a double row of God knows how many more brass buttons. In this day and age to be expected to wear such a monstrosity was ridiculous, but I had to have it with me at all times since it was considered part of my uniform. It was at Flatholm that I discovered the use for such a coat ... on the bed to supplement the small rectangular blankets that were issued. With no heating in the bedrooms the old coat was a godsend.

First Aid was administered by the Principal Keeper with the aid of *The Ship Captain's Medical Guide*. The interior of the medical chest was divided into squares, each holding a square-shaped bottle with a glass stopper covered with muslin and tied around the neck with string. In the lower part of the chest was a drawer containing a set of scales for weighing out the necessary medicinal powder to make up potions, and, believe it or not, scalpels! However, in reality minor injuries were dealt with by medicinal plasters, etc. and any illness or major injury reported by radio and arrangements made to bring the patient ashore. With the issue of standardised First Aid boxes the chests were eventually discontinued.

In March 1967 a shipping disaster at Land's End was to have repercussions around the world in the way oil tankers were handled. A tanker named *Torrey Canyon*, one of the first 'supertankers' designed to carry thousands of tons of crude oil ran aground on rocks between the Seven Stones Lightvessel and the Longships Lighthouse at Land's End, Cornwall, spilling over 100,000 tons of crude oil into the sea. The devastation to the environment of a disaster on this scale was unprecedented and the government brought in the Air Force to bomb the ship with napalm in an attempt to set the oil on fire and burn it off. This was not 100% successful and pollution of our coasts went on for a long time. The lessons learned from this incident were, however, applied worldwide in the design of ships and the transportation of huge cargoes of oil. (Ships nowadays far exceed the size of the *Torrey Canyon*, but in 1967 she was considered an enormous vessel.)

A return to Bull Point brought about a pleasant surprise, as instead of the old caravan I'd had to occupy previously, I now had a one-room bedsit in the junior keeper's house (he received an allowance for forgoing one of his rooms). I still didn't have a bathroom, but with advance notice I could arrange to use that of the keeper's family. However, I still had to use the chemical loo up the yard.

At the time of my visit work was in progress on the construction of a bungalow for the Principal Keeper in what had been the garden area. Its completion would allow the junior keeper to eventually move into what was now the PK's house, leaving his limited quarters available for SAKs and maintenance personnel.

Precarious positions

Following Bull Point I did a tour of duty at Lynmouth Foreland Lighthouse near Lynton, another shore-based station. It was deemed too isolated for families, so was manned by relieving crews in the same manner as an offshore station. My colleagues here were Frank Harris PK, and Alan Callaghan AK. Lynmouth was a strange station as it was a split-level building clinging precariously to the cliffside, and because it sat behind a mountain and faced north it received very little sunshine, so the interior always appeared dark. Although a very isolated station it did, however, have its own electrical supply provided by diesel generators for the living quarters and one of the new triple-frequency fog signals. The main navigation light was at that point still provided by a 35-mm IOB oil lamp mounted inside a beautiful rotating First Order optic of eight panels in two groups of four, and driven by a weight-driven clock.

Strumble Head was another isolated shore-based light I was to visit (it sat on the summit of a small rocky islet connected to the mainland by a footbridge) near Fishguard in South Wales, that was manned as a rock station with relieving crews. My colleagues here were Terry Creswell AK as the senior keeper, and Alan Wilson AK. This was quite a comfortable station as a bathroom had recently been installed, and it also had an electricity supply from the mains, albeit a temporary one installed in 1946, but it made life much more pleasant. The lantern contained a First Order lens mounted on a mercury trough and with the standard weight-driven clock. Its fog signal, however, came as a surprise as it was from explosives (the first one I had encountered). The explosive charge was a small package

Strumble Head

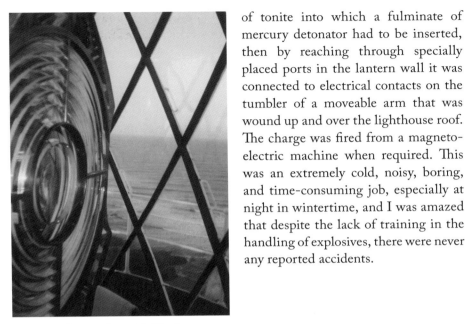

Lens at Strumble Head

of tonite into which a fulminate of mercury detonator had to be inserted, then by reaching through specially placed ports in the lantern wall it was connected to electrical contacts on the tumbler of a moveable arm that was wound up and over the lighthouse roof. The charge was fired from a magneto-electric machine when required. This was an extremely cold, noisy, boring, and time-consuming job, especially at night in wintertime, and I was amazed that despite the lack of training in the handling of explosives, there were never any reported accidents.

OPTICAL LENS ORDERS

Chance Bros of Birmingham became the main British manufacturer and supplier of lighthouse equipment in the second half of the 19th century who adopted and developed the Fresnel lens system. Standard optical systems were developed as 'Orders' which related to the focal distance of the optical panel from the light source.

The Chance Bros' Orders were:

Hyper-radial	1330	mm
Meso-radial	1125	mm
First Order	920	mm
Second Order	700	mm
Third Order	500	mm
Fourth Order	250	mm
Fifth Order	187.5	mm
Sixth Order	150	mm

The irregular placing of the panels added another characteristic, that of group flashing.

EXPLOSIVE FOG SIGNAL

Thomas Matthews, Engineer-in-Chief to Trinity House, devised an explosive fog signal jib that could be wound up and over the lighthouse lantern roof where the explosive charges could be fired safely and without causing damage to the building. For further details and illustrations see Appendix 3.

Matthews also adapted the Kitson PVB lamp prior to David Hood's IOB (see Appendix 4).

3

A *surprise promotion*

On 31 July whilst on duty at Strumble Head I learned that I was to be promoted to Assistant Keeper to the Wolf Rock Lighthouse in the English Channel, a place notorious for overdue reliefs due to a constant ground swell. Despite this I was pleased because it meant a considerable rise in pay. As a permanent crew member working a duty period of two months on the lighthouse followed by one month on leave I would have a reasonable certainty of knowing when I would be home and away. With that stability I could at last plan some family events, so life was now looking a little better. My promotion was later confirmed by letter, when I was astonished to learn that I was actually to be posted to Sark Lighthouse in the Channel Islands and not to the Wolf (I was to find out later that as a consequence of his breaking the rules, the Superintendent had assigned another colleague to the Wolf instead of me), so I was fortunate in avoiding one of the most notorious rock stations on the south coast. Sark Lighthouse was a most desirable and almost unheard of first posting for a newly-appointed Assistant Keeper so I was very fortunate. The traditional procedure within the Service was for newly-appointed assistants to be sent to rock towers, and then after a time transferred to the more comfortable island stations before going back to the rocks on promotion to Principal, then finally the islands again or perhaps a shore-based family station from where he could retire. So for me to be given a plum position as a first station was very unusual, which didn't go amiss among the more senior keepers.

Before I could take up my appointment at Sark I still had to finish my current round of duty (but now in the rank of Assistant Keeper) and was immediately sent by ship (*Stella*) on a regular relief to the South Light at Lundy Island for one month.

Landing at the South Light was different to that at the north end. Here I was landed on a small beach in the south-east of the island directly below the lighthouse because, as the lighthouse was 200 feet above, it was necessary to negotiate a dangerously unstable footpath along a loose shale hillside and then climb a series of wooden steps pegged to the high cliffside to reach it – a hard

South Light at Lundy (Courtesy Chris Foulds)

and arduous climb. Luckily all the food and equipment was lifted directly out of the boat on a wire hoist and was on station when I arrived. The South Light was a much brighter proposition than its counterpart at the north end. It was light and airy and had recently been modernised with electricity supplied from diesel generators. It had a bathroom (although it retained its chemical toilet outside), hot and cold water on tap, and a heating system, so was a far nicer and more comfortable station to work at. My colleagues here were Arthur Robertson (Robbie) PK and Jimmy (Gentleman Jim) Thompson AK.

The navigation light was from a single 1,000-watt lamp with a small Fourth Order lens mounted on an electrically driven central pedestal; the compressors for the fog signal were also diesel driven. Being close to the island settlement or village the keepers of the South Light were considered part of the island community, and as such they could occasionally, during their off-duty time, be seen in the bar of the hotel, and on occasions would invite guests of the hotel to visit their station. The rolling green fields of the south end of the island are so different from the rocky outcrops and bracken of the north that this encouraged me to get out and about, especially along the east side. In the summer the cliffs are a beautiful blaze of colour from the rhododendron bushes that proliferate there, and as this was an island I had come to love I enjoyed my stay. On completion of my duty I went home on leave.

Family relocation

During these first 12 months of my service I was, despite being away from home, trying to relocate my family back into our home town so they would be nearer parents and grandparents while I was away, but the sale of one home and the purchase of another fell mostly on my wife's shoulders. By a stroke of good fortune I was at home on leave, not only when the deals were finalised but also for the birth of my second daughter, and I was able to be there to help establish them in our new home.

Although it had been pleasant travelling from one lighthouse to another it was not financially very rewarding as I was only on basic pay unless sent to an offshore station, when I qualified for extra allowances, and I always needed to have ready cash available for food and travelling; expenses for travel were only refunded after each actual journey.

With the above in mind, the news that the results of an investigation into lighthouse keepers' pay and conditions had recommended a substantial pay increase of 30% along with paid return travel between home and appointed lighthouse was absolutely terrific and would make a tremendous difference. The requirement for a keeper to live within the depot area was also relaxed (but to my knowledge never rescinded), so this was not only very welcome news, but a major improvement on the money front.

Naval attachment

I had been looking forward with great anticipation to travelling to the Channel Islands, but a few days before setting off I received instruction from my new Superintendent at the East Cowes Depot telling me to ignore my previous instructions as I was required to fill a temporary vacancy at Portland breakwater Lighthouse where the Principal Keeper had just retired. I was to stay there until a new one was appointed, when I could pick up my duties at Sark.

The lighthouse at Portland Breakwater is situated inside the Royal Naval Dockyard at Portland in Dorset and is owned and operated by the naval authorities, but the keepers and maintenance crews were supplied by Trinity House and contracted out to the Navy.

Portland Breakwater

As this was a NATO establishment security was tight, so I was issued with a pass that was good for just one entry and one departure, and after undergoing routine security checks at the main gate I was escorted to the dockside where naval ratings in full uniform were waiting to transport me to the lighthouse aboard the Queen's Harbour Master's launch – very posh, all polished woodwork and gleaming brass with big padded cushions inside; transport does not get any better than this, and I was treated like a visiting VIP. The lighthouse stood on the end of a central mole or breakwater marking one of two main entrances to the harbour, and was a tall steel structure braced with steel legs and lattice side braces. Accommodation was provided in a separate building some 100 yards from the tower, and although there was electric light, cooking was done on a solid fuel range which also provided heating. There was a bathroom, but this was in a separate building (a steel turret) some way along the breakwater. The living room/kitchen was of very small proportions; almost all the available floor space was occupied by a square kitchen table and three straight-backed chairs, and even when these were pushed under the table it was difficult to get from one side of the room to the other. When all three men were seated, one of the chair backs was touching a wall, the other the kitchen sink, while the third side had a little more space as it was in front of the main door; the fourth side of the table fronted the cooking range which was so close that the man cooking could actually sit on the table while doing so. All in all, this was a tiny space. Adjoining the kitchen was a bedroom that I shared with the senior keeper Simon Reynolds; a second single bedroom, usually occupied by the Principal Keeper but at present occupied by Jock Cameron AK, had its access from outside on the other side of the building. Encased in scaffold, the lighthouse was just undergoing conversion from oil to gas, so we had the company of several Trinity House mechanics who, thankfully, had separate living quarters along the breakwater. The original light in the tower had been from a 35-mm IOB, but this was removed within days of my arrival and an emergency substitute battery light fitted to the domed roof to allow the existing lighting equipment, plus the air and fuel containers, to be removed to make space for the new equipment. Throughout the work our duties became very disrupted and depended very much on what stage the mechanics were at, but they were mainly to look after the emergency light and its batteries until a new gas light was installed. The old fog signal bell weighing around six hundredweight and suspended from the side of the tower was carefully removed along with the hand-wound multiplex clockwork mechanism that drove it and the lens, and it was sad to see this beautiful piece of engineering dismantled and destroyed just for its scrap value. With hindsight this would have been a star attraction in any museum today. Being isolated on this central mole on the seaward side of the harbour there was nowhere to walk to apart from down its length (half a mile), but this was not pleasant because of the amount of rubble strewn about from the many damaged and vandalised buildings, so much of our time was spent in or near the quarters watching ships and boats moving around the harbour, or watching the mechanics at work. One afternoon while working in the kitchen I was becoming puzzled as to why the daylight was gradually disappearing, when to my amazement a huge black conning tower appeared in the window almost in my face and continued to rise from the depths. Apparently directly alongside the breakwater at that point was a deep submarine diving pit; not something you see every day.

With the arrival of the new PK, Harry Fenn, I had anticipated being released from the station to take up my position at Sark, but while I was on leave my colleague Jock, the Assistant Keeper at the breakwater resigned, and I was ordered to return there to fill in until his replacement was found. I remained on temporary detachment at Portland Breakwater on regular shifts until December 1967, and was fortunate in being home for another Christmas.

Channel Islands

Christmas 1967 was special as I now had a second daughter who was only three months old; so it was with mixed feelings that, my leave over and the joys of Christmas barely fading, I received, five months after my appointment, the long-awaited orders to join the relief for Sark, where I could settle into the long-awaited routine of two months at the lighthouse followed by one month at home.

I was expected to travel to the islands by the cheapest means possible, which was by train to Weymouth and then ferry to Guernsey, and from there a further ferry to Sark. However, by taking into account the subsistence allowance for the longer journey I found that the difference between travelling overland and flying was almost negligible, so I opted to fly and pay the difference myself. On 5 January 1968 I finally began my first official journey to Sark. Taking the BA shuttle from Liverpool to Heathrow I joined the Guernsey flight. Arriving mid-morning I found Guernsey overcast, wet and cold, and after organising overnight accommodation in St Peter Port I got on with the task of shopping and arranging for my supplies to be packed and delivered to the harbour the following morning.

The ferry for Sark was a passenger boat with an internal passenger saloon and seating on the open upper decks which, despite the time of year I took advantage of, and with calm seas I enjoyed the one-hour passage to Sark passing the smaller islands of Herm and Jethou.

The approach into Maseline Harbour took us directly beneath my new posting, Point Robert Lighthouse, a split-level building clinging to the hillside overlooking the pier where we would dock. On the dockside I was greeted by a rough-looking chap who introduced himself as John Perry, the Trinity House agent for the lighthouse who said he would take me to the lighthouse on his tractor when he'd collected his goods from the ship. As I perched precariously on the mudguard over the big tractor wheel we climbed the steep roadway from the harbour to the comparatively flat top of the island, then along the gravel-packed roads to the lighthouse entrance gate high above the building. A narrow pathway begins the approach to a long straight flight of granite stone steps to the lighthouse, and in several trips, laden with boxes and bags, I eventually managed to get all my belongings down into the yard. As the lantern of the lighthouse was on a level with the lower steps I can recall seeing the Principal Keeper inside taking down the curtains in preparation for lighting the light, so entering my new station I found my way up to the lantern to introduce myself. My colleagues here were Norman Wakely the PK, who was a Sarkie and lived on the island, and Bill Humphries AK who, like me, was from the mainland.

The lighthouse is built on two levels, the upper floor containing the living quarters, which consist of kitchen, living room, three bedrooms and bathroom,

Point Robert, Sark (Courtesy Chris Foulds)

and for the first time since joining the Service I had the surprise of seeing a couple of new cottage-style fireside chairs and an officially issued television set! The lower floor consisted of a workshop and engine room along with the fog signal air receivers. The fog signal here was a compressed-air 'reed' signal powered from 5-hp Hornsby oil engines, miniatures of those I had learned to drive at Flatholm Lighthouse, and as usual everything was shining like a new pin. The main navigation light was from a 75-mm IOB oil lamp, and the large lens was powered by a hand-wound clockwork mechanism with which I was familiar, but the living quarters had electric light powered from the island's mains supply; water was supplied from a deep borehole on the top of the island.

Sark is the smallest of the four major Channel Islands and is about 80 miles south of England and 20 miles west of France; it has an area of less than two square miles with a population of 550. There are no motor cars on the island, transport being either by tractor-drawn trailer, or the more popular horse and carriage. During the first couple of months I found my way around the island, its bays and two harbours, meeting many nice people, some who were islanders born and bred, and others who had chosen to retire there.

Being a fully-fledged Assistant Keeper at an appointed station meant life was much more leisurely and less hectic than being an SAK when I was expected to travel at a moment's notice, as I was now in a dedicated routine of two months on station and one month ashore, so I could plan other activities around those dates. My colleagues were all responsible men, each knowing the importance of what he was doing and, although there was a Principal Keeper, each man did his job without supervision.

The keepers had many hobbies. In some cases these allowed the men to fulfil an ambition, in others simply to do or make something of interest for themselves. As long as it wasn't a noisy interest it could be worked on at any time of the day or night. I was to meet some who knitted, crocheted or did tapestry work, and it was these and many other hobbies that I was to take up myself with varying degrees of success (but that would be in the future). My hobby as an SAK had been making soft animals and simple wooden toys for my children along with cross stitching, interesting activities for which materials were light and easy to carry. I was eventually to see just about everything you can think of as a hobby being pursued by one man or another. It was the general introduction of television sets to all lighthouses that killed off most (but not all) of these interests.

During their off-duty time the keepers, as part of the island community, would frequently be asked by residents to help out with various odd jobs, which could be anything from taking a horse to the blacksmith, painting, replacing a window or simply delivering a hire bicycle to someone, and on occasion (after training) to drive a horse and carriage, all of these we were only too willing to do as it gave us an outside interest.

No sooner had I settled into island life than in the March I was shocked to receive notification that I was required for temporary duty as Keeper-in-Charge at Alderney Lighthouse during the period May to September, as their senior keeper was due to go on a detached duty to Europa Point Lighthouse at Gibraltar. It was intended that I should spend my first month of duty at Alderney followed by my second at Sark. Now here was I, a junior keeper with less than two years' service, and only eight months as an Assistant Keeper, being asked to go to a completely strange station and take charge of it and its crew in the opposite turn to the Principal Keeper! I don't remember how I felt about that (peeved probably), but I'm sure I wasn't flattered.

EGGS AND SHELLS

For my first tour of duty at Alderney I flew to Guernsey, where I was to connect with the flight for Alderney. Checking in for the flight I was amused to find that not only was my baggage weighed, but I was also asked to step onto the scales and take with me the six eggs I was carrying in a paper bag. The short flight was in an eight seater Islander aircraft that did the regular run to and from Alderney, and passengers were seated according to their weight to maintain the balance of the aircraft. As this was my first flight I got to sit up front with the pilot, from where the island approach was quite spectacular. Subsequent flights were to be equally spectacular and the views of the island in clear weather breathtakingly beautiful.

Alderney Lighthouse stands on the beach at Quenard Point on the north-east side of the island and is a huge single-storey station with an extremely tall black-and-white striped tower.

On arrival for my first duty as Keeper-in-Charge I found that the Principal Keeper had already left, which was apparently usual practice because of flight timings, and on station waiting to greet me were three SAKs ... three trainees!

Quenard Point, Alderney (Courtesy Chris Foulds)

What a start, here I was on a strange station with three men who had even less knowledge of it than I had. A tour of the lighthouse showed thankfully that I was familiar with all the equipment as there was a 75-mm IOB lamp, and the large First Order lens was driven by clockwork; the fog engines were the big 22-hp Hornsbys I had driven before, so no huge surprises there, and after setting the watches and settling in, we all got on with what was required.

The official watchkeeping position for the man on duty in most lighthouses was the service room directly below the lantern, (a) to check the light character and regularly wind the clockwork mechanism, anything from every 30 minutes to every two hours or so, and (b) to be on hand if anything should happen to the light, especially fire, but because there were no facilities or heating in the service room many men kept their watch in the living room, keeping an eye on the light via a strategically placed mirror in the window. At any sign of the light fading, or any other visual problem the watchman was up the tower pretty quickly. With the introduction of diesel engines, television and comfortable easy chairs it became standard practice, almost without exception, for the watchkeeping to be transferred to the living room.

My first turn of duty at Alderney went fairly smoothly despite the inexperience of us all, and like elsewhere when off duty, I had plenty of time to have a good look around the island. Alderney is very much bigger than Sark with a larger population and a town centre (St Ann's) with cars and other road transport, but with no MOT requirement on the island the condition of many of the privately owned cars left a lot to be desired. There was, however, a bus service with a stop right outside the lighthouse gate which was very handy for getting around. Because of its strategic position the island has in the past been heavily fortified, and many of the old defensive forts still stand, as does the proliferation of concrete gun emplacements and pillboxes of the German occupation during the Second World War. Some of them tower several storeys high and, having proved to be virtually indestructible, have become a dominant feature of the local landscape. There was also the crumbling remnants of an out of bounds Second World War concentration camp surrounded by coils of rusting barbed wire, so there remained much to see of the island's turbulent history.

An elderly neighbour living in a nearby cottage was a frequent visitor to the lighthouse bringing various fruits and vegetables from his garden. On one of our return visits to him he proudly showed us his 'cobbled' courtyard of inverted German artillery shells, which was certainly different and no doubt unique, but with a gasp of surprise my companion, an ex-army man, quickly pointed out that some of the shells were still primed and were in effect unexploded bombs... panic!

One of the pleasurable memories of being at Alderney was the ship *Queen Mary* as she passed Alderney on her final voyage out of England on her way to Long Beach, California. As a parting gesture she came close inshore and gave the lighthouse a farewell salute of a couple of long blasts on her funnel whistles. She had been sold to the Americans for use as a floating hotel and tourist attraction. I for one appreciated the gesture and took it as an acknowledgement of the fact that the lighthouse (along with others, of course) had kept her safe during her life in UK waters, so it was a fond farewell. The Captain of the *Queen Mary* for this voyage was Captain John Treasure Jones, and I recalled that way back in 1958 he and I had joined a Cunard ship together, he for his first command and I on my first ship as his bridge boy.

First Christmas apart

Having resumed my normal relief schedule at Sark I found I was to be on duty at the lighthouse for the forthcoming Christmas, so my PK, Norman, invited my wife and children over to stay at his family home on the island for the holiday when I returned for that duty. Having my family on the island for several weeks prior to Christmas was a wonderful experience for us all and we spent a lot of time out and about discovering the sights of the island, but sadly just before Christmas my wife decided it was time that she and the children returned home and asked me to make arrangements for their boat passage and return flight; so we spent our first Christmas as a family apart.

During the summer of 1969 I was again requested to carry out temporary duty at Alderney Lighthouse, and it was during my final tour of duty there that I fell foul of the District Superintendent. During an official annual inspection visit by the Elder Brethren I had an informal chat with the chairman of the committee explaining that I was having a few problems with the amount of extra personnel on station. In addition to the three keepers there were three Trinity House engineers in residence removing the old oil engines and installing new high-speed diesels, two plumbers in the process of installing a central heating system, and then six contract painters had turned up wanting accommodation as they were to paint the entire building inside and out. All these people wanted to occupy the various spaces in and around the station, but as we had no proper accommodation for them, and they would require the use of our facilities, kitchen, bathroom, and living room, etc., I had, on the Principal Keeper's instructions, refused them permission (apart from the engineers) to stay on station. Taking exception to my refusal to house them these men were at every opportunity being bloody minded and making life difficult for myself and my colleagues. Being assured that my concerns were noted, I wasn't unduly worried, and I certainly wasn't prepared for what happened next.

Early the following morning my Superintendent arrived at the station in a foul temper demanding to know why I had discussed the station's problems with the Elder Brethren instead of himself, as apparently he had been instructed to 'get out there and get the problem sorted'. When I had confided in the chairman I certainly hadn't expected him to go and order the Superintendent to come down immediately and sort the problem. Anyway, within days of the Superintendent's visit I was notified that at the end of my duty I was to be transferred back to the mainland and reassigned to the Swansea District. So I didn't get the chance to return to Sark to say goodbye to all the wonderful people I had met there, which was a big disappointment.

4

Against the odds

Family times

My new posting was to be Hartland Point...well, well, well, there's a thing, a station I knew so well where my family and I would occupy the married quarters on a full-time basis. My wife was delighted with the news, and we looked forward to the move and to being together, but because of the difficulties in arranging mutual removal dates with the various transport companies it was eventually nine weeks (early November) before the relevant transfers took place allowing us to travel.

After a long and difficult journey to Devon with two small children we were delighted to finally arrive at our new home, but my reception there was not quite as I had expected. My new Principal Keeper, Ron Smith, made it abundantly clear at our first meeting that he did not want me on his station. In fact his very first words to me were 'I'll have you shifted', meaning of course that he would be instrumental in having me transferred elsewhere. To say that I was staggered beyond belief is no exaggeration: I hadn't a clue as to what I'd done wrong. I had never met the man before in my life. Despite my annoyance I was now too tired to take up the point with him, but that was me certainly told. My second colleague, Assistant Keeper Tony Homewood, was as shocked at the situation as I was, and he went on to become a good friend and ally.

I was however determined to find out what had prompted my PK's anger. It was some weeks later after we had settled in, that I received a phone call from the District Clerk, Mr Jaeger, which was always a pleasure. What he had to say, however, was a bit of a bombshell. 'St Ann's' was all he said. Instantly I knew he was telling me that I was being considered for transfer to another station, and my initial thought was 'This is the influence of Ron Smith at work', but I was not going to give him the satisfaction of getting his own way, and I was certainly not going to disappear as easily as that. Having heard my gasp of surprise Mr Jaeger simply said 'that's OK, that's all I want to know, I take it you are not interested'.

I was furious that one man thought he could pick and choose who joined him on station, as I had always understood that transfers were ordered by the Board and not by PKs. The system could not afford to have stations run by cliques to the detriment of other keepers, and I would not condone it by accepting a transfer. I was also dismayed to learn that it had been my previous Superintendent who had telephoned Ron prior to my arrival to say that he had 'a trouble maker' coming to his station; so much for men in authority and the creation of a reputation!

The accommodation provided at Hartland was a first-floor flat situated above the engine room, and with three bedrooms, living room and kitchen it was quite large. A bathroom and separate toilet were located off the landing above the stairs. All rooms, with the exception of bathroom and kitchen, were painted in magnolia gloss, which was deemed to be a 'service standard'. As this showed every little blemish in the plasterwork where over the years alterations and patches had been made, it wasn't the most desired decoration. During our time here my wife and I campaigned at every opportunity for permission to decorate it ourselves with wallpaper, but this was against company policy as each dwelling had to be of 'service standard', so that personnel knew exactly what to expect of their quarters when they moved in, thereby saving the company money with each transfer by not having to redecorate.

From the living room window we had a magnificent view of Lundy Island 11 miles away, and a treat in store for us in the future was the many beautiful sunsets we would witness. It is, however, said that 'all good things come with a price', and we came to learn in time the price for having these beautiful views; directly below the living room windows were the trumpets of the station foghorn, and directly below us, the engine room. When the fog signal was in operation the heat from the engines became oppressive up in the flat, and as it couldn't be dispersed by opening the window because of the raucous sound of the signal, we were caught between a rock and a hard place, so to speak. The simplest method of avoiding this dilemma was, when I was off duty, to get away from the place altogether. Thankfully it didn't happen too often.

TRANSPORTS OF DELIGHT

Not being able to drive was a pain. If we were to have any independence I had to have a car so learning to drive became a priority. Because of the isolation of the lighthouse each driving lesson was scheduled for several hours, as it was necessary to make the long drive into Bideford or Barnstaple for experience of traffic lights, roundabouts, crossings, etc., so in addition to myself there would also be another learner driver in the car, and we would split the time between us, the non-driving learner benefiting from any comments passed to the actual driver. This was a system that worked well, and the instructor was very proficient, which led to an early test and licence. Having a car gave us much more freedom to come and go as we pleased during my off-duty hours, and as the spring grew into summer we ventured further afield throughout the county, and into Somerset and Cornwall, having leisurely picnics in some lovely places.

DIGGING FOR VICTORY

The water supply for the lighthouse was provided from a borehole on nearby farmland, but had previously been rainwater supplied from a large sloping concrete area of ground. The land surrounding it had been used by previous generations of keepers as gardens, but it now appeared not to have been used since the 'Dig for Victory' campaign of the last war, and was in a pretty rough state. With a lot of spare off-duty time I decided to resurrect one of these abandoned gardens; despite the difficulty of clearing the thick undergrowth I was eventually able to get the ground into a condition where I could sow seeds and plant young seedlings. With the garden growing well it was nice to have our own fresh vegetables, and I recall that one Christmas Day the garden produced all the fresh vegetables we needed for dinner.

We found that life for us at Hartland was very pleasant, and I suppose it was quite stress free. The added freedom of being mobile enabled us to do many things as a family that hadn't been possible before because I was away from home. I think the following extract of an article by my wife, published by the Association of Lighthouse Keepers in its quarterly journal in March 1994, will give some idea of just what life was like there.

> ...The lighthouse is in a beautiful part of North Devon, about 5 miles from the small village of Hartland and quite close to the very popular and picturesque village of Clovelly. It is approached along narrow country lanes with high hedge rows, the road finally ending at a local farm where access was only permitted to the Coastguard Station and the lighthouse. The farmer would however allow visitors during the summer months to cross his land to park on the headland with its magnificent sea views,

but for this privilege a toll was payable. From the farm, the road down to the lighthouse became very steep and narrow, being cut into the cliff face, the rock on one side rising quite dramatically to over 200ft, and the cliff on the seaward side having a drop of the same to the beach below, at first sight this can be quite hair raising. The road runs around the headland dropping all the time, and the lighthouse doesn't appear until the very last moment, when suddenly it appears perched on a small rock plateau surrounded by a white boundary wall. Due to the small space available the station is by necessity very compact, comprising of only one building which is divided into individual dwellings for the keepers [and families], engine room and attached tower.

The buildings stand in an enclosed yard area, and the most obvious thing you notice is that there are no gardens, in fact there is not a single blade of grass to be seen [not even a weed]. After leaving a house with a large garden and play area this does not appear to be an ideal situation to be bringing two small children to I suppose, but the idea of being together as a family was to override this. After settling into our new home it soon became apparent that if we were to have any life outside the station then the first priority was to learn to drive and obtain a car, otherwise we would be seeing an awful lot of the place. On my previous visit the other keepers and their wives had occasionally taken us out with them in their cars, but now as permanent residents it was a different matter, and if we were to be independent then we needed transport.

Our companions on this lonely outpost were the Principal Keeper and his wife [Ron and Gladys Smith] (their children having now left home for a life outside the Service), and the Senior Assistant Keeper and his wife [Tony and Daphne Homewood]. There were at that time no other children on the station. During the three years I spent there the other wives taught me how to make jam from the fruits of the hedgerows, the preserving of fresh country fruit, and the making of chutney, pickling, and the pressing of tongue! [Gladys had been a keeper's wife all her married life and was well versed in the preserving of food, as in the early days that was the only way Ron could keep food on the lighthouses he served at as there were no fridges. Daphne, being a local girl, had been brought up in the ways of country folk, and had been used to seeing her grandparents and parents making use of all these skills.]

Once we had obtained a car, off duty days saw us away from the station on trips of discovery around the county, and having come from a city environment I was thoroughly enjoying the open space and freshness of the countryside, visiting beautiful towns and villages I had only read about before. Despite the isolation of the station, I never grew tired of the silence which was broken only by the screeching of gulls (apart from the necessary boom of the fog signal), or of watching the sea break against the cliffs sending great plumes of spray into the air, or of storms, which could be so severe that giant boulders were shifted along the beach, and one of the great delights was to see a dark night sky lit only by streaks of lightning, or by the stars and moon without the reflection of street lights.

Two children were to be born to the other assistant keeper and his wife while we lived here, and these, along with our own children were to become playmates. When our eldest daughter Paula was five years old she attended the local primary school; the school bus would arrive at the lighthouse to pick her up after having called at outlying farms first, but due to the danger of the [lighthouse] approach road the bus would only call to the entrance gate which was a ¼ mile away behind the headland, so each morning and afternoon we had the long trek up and down the road because the gate wasn't visible from the lighthouse, and we would have to be there in good time, and at times the wind would be so strong we would be knocked off our feet, and there was the ever present danger of the unfenced cliff top. It was also not unusual to find that large falls of rock had blocked the approach road, so extreme caution was always necessary. Sunday school and birthday parties were great fun, each Sunday morning Gordon would take the children by car to the village church, collecting other children from a farm on the way. When we first arrived at the station this was done by a Mr Huggins the local garage owner and church warden, but his great age had caused his retirement.

On birthdays, school friends would come to us direct from school on the bus, but we always had to inform the bus company in advance of pick-ups so that they could plan their schedule. There was always great excitement among the children at coming down to the lighthouse, and afterwards we had the task of taking them all home, some of which were spread far and wide. When our girls were invited to parties it would not be unusual to do a 20 mile round trip ... so much for close friends!

The article ends with the following quote from her concluding thoughts ...

On the plus side, Gordon was at home, or available 24 hours a day, although I can appreciate that it is not every couple who are capable of being together all that time.

Provisions of milk, eggs, poultry, vegetables and fruit came straight from the farms, and simple things like shopping, or exchanging library books was done on off duty days and became a day out for the family. So I suppose a close family bond was developed because we did more activities together as a family, most of which would probably have been done by only one partner outside the Service....Both Gordon and Tony submitted requests for transfers at the same time, and within a short time were moved to rock stations within 4 weeks of each other, and so ended our only stay at a land station. Certainly an experience I will always remember.

Throughout all these jolly times my relationship with Ron Smith remained at the status quo, I doing as I was told, and he not unduly pressurising me, and to be fair, although we didn't get on, he was always good with the children and polite with my wife ... it was just me he didn't like.

As an accessible shore station the lighthouse was a popular attraction for visitors, opening on six days of the week throughout the spring and summer. The keepers took their annual leave at the end of the season in late September, each keeper in turn by seniority, so being the junior man I was the last to go, but having to take my leave so late in the year, and in a four week block, didn't really suit, and against my PK's wishes I applied for permission to take my leave in future years in two two-week periods at varying times in the year, a request which, much to Ron Smith's annoyance, was granted.

Negotiations between Trinity House and the keepers' union brought about a change in working practices whereby the keepers no longer had to work the extra hours each morning outside their watch-keeping hours, which meant that we now had a lot more free time, but I fear this didn't go down too well with my PK who demanded that two men be on station at all times. Representation to my union and the Superintendent confirmed the regulation, so Ron lost the day, and we were free to leave the station when off duty.

A QUEEN, A PIRATE AND TWO FLOWERPOT MEN

In June 1972 my younger daughter and my colleague Tony's young son were entered in the village playgroup fancy dress competition as the Queen of Hearts, and a Pirate. Both costumes were superb and the kids looked a treat, and they came away with a first and second prize brilliant. Flushed with this success, we entered all three children into the village Summer Carnival as Bill & Ben the Flowerpot Men and Little Weed, based on the popular children's television series at that time. We borrowed a new Morris pick-up truck from the local farmer and decorated it as a garden scene, surrounding the outside with a painted paper wall, a greenhouse gable behind the cab, and crossed fork and spade across the radiator, and with the children dressed in their costumes of cardboard plant pots, wash baskets disguised as giant pots, and all the hanging house plants we could find trailing off the back it looked absolutely terrific and we knew we had a winner. I drove the float slowly in procession around the village and we could tell by the reaction of the people lining the streets that they were delighted with our efforts, and subsequently at the judging we were awarded first prize.

It must have been in the autumn of 1972 that Ron Smith announced he had applied for a transfer to Withernsea Lighthouse on Humberside, which was a man and wife station, meaning that only he and his wife Gladys would operate it, and his replacement at Hartland would be Jack Burrage PK. Ron duly departed (alone) for training at his new post, leaving his wife to co-ordinate the packing and removal of their furniture, but before she and their possessions were ready to follow him we were staggered to learn that for one reason or another he had changed his mind and had requested a return to Hartland!

With the start of the new school term in September our youngest daughter was accepted at the local primary school, and she and her elder sister cheerfully boarded the school bus hand in hand each morning, and now that they were both at school my wife and I had a lot more free time just to shop and visit friends in the area. We just had to remember to be back at the lighthouse in time for the school bus, or perhaps, if we were in the locality, pick the girls up from school ourselves.

Damaged Bull Point with temporary light tower

Landslip and collapse

On the morning of 24 September 1972 we received the dramatic news that Bull Point Lighthouse had suffered catastrophic damage in a landslip. Apparently over 50 feet of the headland on which it stands had suddenly given way, causing the engine room to severely subside and break up and the tower to list out of the perpendicular. Thankfully the cottages were unaffected by this initial collapse and the families were immediately evacuated, unscathed. A rapidly deployed workforce from Trinity House was quickly on the scene to salvage what equipment they could from the wreckage, and then quickly transported an old abandoned light tower (Bideford Lighthouse) from its original site at Saunton Sands to Bull Point. Using the salvaged equipment, a temporary light was made available within 24 hours. Meanwhile a lightvessel had been prepared at Swansea and was towed out and positioned off the headland at Morethoe to provide a fog signal until one could be established ashore. Two years later a new lighthouse (the present one) was opened several hundred yards further inland.

With my children now at school and having found other interests outside the lighthouse, my wife and I, over a period of time, came to the conclusion that the isolation of the station was not beneficial to them and that they should really have more contact with other children, so we gave great thought to our moving on. We decided that moving to another land station wouldn't help, so I should apply for a transfer to a rock station and we would buy a house of our own elsewhere. While waiting for a response to this request I was astounded to be informed that our campaign for the flat to be wallpapered had finally been given approval and that we could choose a paper up to X pounds per roll and that the company painters would hang it; a change of heart, but sadly not one we were to benefit from. Within just a couple of weeks of my transfer request I learned that, it too, had been granted and I was to go to Coquet Island in Northumberland.

BRITAIN'S TALLEST LIGHTHOUSES

Bishop Rock's Isles of Scilly – 197 feet
Eddystone, south-west of Plymouth – 168 feet

5

Northumberland

Horns or frying pans

October 1972 brought the day of my departure, but as I had not been granted any leave to find alternative accommodation I had no choice but to leave my wife and children behind at the lighthouse. I was to be away for eight weeks so there was no chance that they could leave Hartland until my return. Despite the fact that I was having to leave early that morning if I was to reach Northumberland at a reasonable hour, my PK had insisted I carry out my midnight to 4 a.m. watch, so no concession from him right to the end.

My destination was the small seaside town of Amble, about 30 miles north of Newcastle-upon-Tyne, where I had to report to the Trinity House agent and boatman. After reaching the town I had to obtain food supplies for my first four weeks and make arrangements for the second four weeks' supplies to be sent out to me. The following morning I boarded an open launch at the harbour for the crossing to Coquet Island, passing the sad sight of the broken wooden piers of a once thriving coal exporting industry. Once clear of the harbour it was possible to see the low-lying island of Coquet with its square lighthouse tower about three-quarters of a mile away. After 25–30 minutes we pulled into a stone landing pier where the keepers were waiting to throw us the mooring ropes, and it was there that I saw the familiar face of the Principal Keeper, Fred Jones, the Principal I had last seen at North Lundy when I was an SAK in training, and here I was now to be his senior hand.

The island is low lying and extends to about 16 acres. It was leased from the Duke of Northumberland in 1840 for the purpose of building a lighthouse, the tower of which was erected above the ruins of an existing monastic building that had been mentioned in a 'List of Castles' in 1415, so it has a very old pedigree

Coquet Island Light

indeed. As such it is Grade 2 listed, therefore the original lower section of what is now the lighthouse tower is kept as natural unpainted stone, while the top is painted white. The living quarters, with four bedrooms on two floors, are built around the base of the tower, with my room on the first floor having terrific views out over the water towards the shore and the harbour. Oil lamps for lighting in the living quarters were the order of the day out here, but one concession came in the form of small easy chairs and a television powered from a car battery, which was sufficient for watching the news and sporting programmes. The domestic water supply was stored rainwater collected from the roof. The main navigation light was provided by a 75-mm IOB lamp, a clockwork-powered hood being lowered to cover it at regular intervals to produce an occulting light. The lens, dated 1835, was fixed with a wide central belt section which, owing to the poor quality of glass and the airborne residue of oil from the lamps, had a greenish tinge, and many of its prisms had been chipped and damaged over the years, all of which made cleaning very difficult. Situated on a mezzanine floor part way up

IOB lamp and hood (Courtesy Chris Foulds)

the tower were three Douglass wick lamps with parabolic reflectors that formed a separate sector light to indicate a passage inshore; two of these lamps showed a red light, and one white. The Coquet at this time was the sole remaining station in the Service to use Douglass wick lamps, and to maintain a bright light it was necessary to keep the circular silver-plated reflectors highly polished with jewellers' rouge, a fine red powder made up into a paste that created a shine without scratching. Through the night each of these lights in turn had to be extinguished, and using a

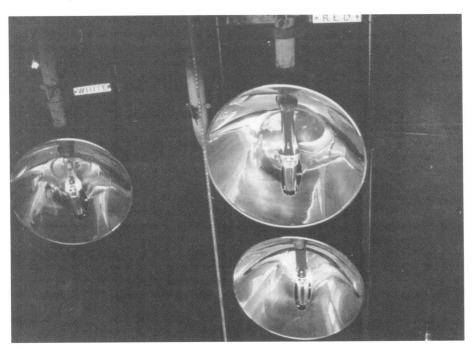

Wick lamps at Coquet (Courtesy Chris Foulds)

special pair of scissors a hard crust was trimmed from the wick before relighting. If this wasn't done properly, or if neglected then the light slowly dimmed to the point of being useless.

One of the drawbacks of living on an oil-powered lighthouse was that we suffered from a terrific amount of condensation. Through the night moisture formed on the walls then trickled down to the floor and down the long spiral staircase to form a puddle at the base of the tower, which meant that regular mopping up was required to prevent slips or falls, and during the winter months, with no heating in the tower, the moisture occasionally actually froze on the lantern and service room walls! Settling into the usual routine of an offshore station with its oil lamp, clockwork mechanism and explosives fog signal came easily enough, as did looking after the paraffin fridge, but an additional piece of equipment I had not used since training was the radio telephone, which I would now have to use as part of my watch routine to send and receive messages via a coast radio station. When using the radio you had to follow the correct protocol and procedure, using the correct radio frequencies, or you couldn't get anywhere, and as this was also the only means of communication with the shore it was important to get it right. Every hour on the hour there was a 'quiet period', a time when all licensed radio users were obliged to monitor the emergency channel for any emergency calls, and immediately following this the coast station would declare a 'traffic list' of those who had telephone calls waiting, and if our name was on it we had to call and ask for a connection. Invariably the lighthouse was given a late connection number depending how much traffic there was, and since there was no way of knowing how long each caller was going to be on air, you just had to sit it out and wait for your turn. The conversation of each caller could be heard by everyone else waiting their turn, so a personal call was not actually a 'personal' one, and on more than one occasion I was to hear the coast station operator interrupt lady callers talking to their husbands out on the oil rigs to say, 'Madam, may I remind that your call can be heard all over the North Sea'!

I wasn't at the station too long before I received a radio call from my wife to say that Trinity House wanted her and the children to 'vacate the property forthwith' as she was holding up the transfer of another keeper, but as we had not been allowed any time in which to make alternative arrangements before I left I felt there was no option but to tell her to remain there until I came home on leave. However, unbeknown to me the Superintendent of that district continued to pressurise her to go, but distressing as it was there was little I could do until I returned home.

During Fred's leave period I was the Keeper-in-Charge at the station and came to realise that Fred ran his station with the minimum of effort and on a minimum of stores, as just about everything except Brasso was in short supply, and this included oil for the lamps and drinking water, each of which had to be carefully monitored.

Some months later I encountered a really serious problem when after an extensive session of sounding for fog I discovered we were running out of explosive charges. The last consignment had been lost at sea during a storm and hadn't been reordered. I therefore had to report the situation via a radio–telephone link to the Superintendent, who was, to say the least, not at all pleased. He was even less pleased when, to his question 'have you anything else to make a noise with?' (meaning a hand-operated Norwegian Horn as supplied to lightvessels and rock towers), he heard me reply 'Only a large frying pan and a spoon, sir'… Oh! why do I open my big mouth sometimes. The outcome was that an emergency stock of explosives had to be flown in by helicopter and I had to submit a report on the situation.

The RAF to the rescue

It was a day or two before Christmas Eve that I travelled back to Hartland after my first eight weeks' duty, and after spending Christmas together in the flat we decided it was time to go, and made arrangements to move into lodgings elsewhere until we could find somewhere to live. We had enjoyed our stay at Hartland and had had some good times, and I'm sure we all have very fond memories of the place. With our furniture in storage it was time to find a new home. After some months of searching when I was on leave we eventually found the one we wanted, and to the delight of the children it didn't have a light on top!

At the crucial time when the contracts had to be signed and exchanged I was away from home, and to await my return would have delayed the purchase and could possibly have led to the loss of the house to another purchaser. Luckily the local RAF came to the rescue by delivering the contracts when next on exercise in the area, allowing time for them to be signed and witnessed and collecting them on their return to base. The big yellow Sea King helicopter landed right outside the lighthouse door and I was passed a large brown envelope. One hour later the documents were on their way back home and we were able to secure the house. Well done the RAF!

Being on a grass-covered island gave plenty of opportunity to get out and about, and when off duty we played cricket and football or simply strolled around the perimeter on a grass track cropped short by the resident hoards of scrawny rabbits. The other residents in abundance were puffins (or sea parrot), the comical black-and-white sea birds with the huge multi-coloured beaks that were to a point tame enough to be approached quite closely; whenever we were working around the landing area they would stand in rows on the high ground watching us, and with constantly bobbing head would appear to take in all we were doing.

Spooks and cooks

Coquet, like many other stations, has a ghost, the story of which was frequently told, and a favourite story relating to it is that of the keeper going to fetch a bucket of coal during the early morning before his colleagues were up and about. The coal was kept in what was once the crypt of an ancient monastery, and I suppose with this in mind and deep in his own thoughts he almost shot through the roof when, as he turned to leave with the coal, he was addressed by a dark hooded figure. It appears that the local boatman had arrived unseen and dropped off the chaplain to the Missions to Seamen who was making a regular but unannounced visit.

I continued to work to the routine of two months on duty and one month at home until 1974 when double manning of lighthouses was introduced, giving us one month on duty followed by one month ashore, a tremendous improvement in working conditions. However, to implement this required a huge intake of new recruits who, to the annoyance of the established keepers, were instantly appointed to the rank of Assistant Keeper. These new recruits, on arrival at the Coquet, were flabbergasted to find its archaic equipment as they hadn't been trained in the use or operation of either oil lamps or explosives. True, there were few of these oil stations now left in service, but while a single oil lamp still existed then surely trainees should be trained in those basics, all of which only underlined my original thoughts about the inadequacy of the training school. With the influx of younger men joining the Service many of them chose to spend their off-duty time in their own company and some of the old traditions began to be questioned. Of greatest effect was their reluctance to fall into the 'cook of the day' routine whereby all three men sat down together to a cooked meal each day, which subsequently led to separate meals being cooked at all times of the day and night.

It was the IRA bombings in Birmingham in 1974 that brought about a tightening of controls in the use of explosives, and after a visit to the island from a government explosives expert Trinity House responded by discontinuing those fog signals where they were still used. Ours at the Coquet was removed within a matter of weeks, to be replaced by two portable diesel-driven generators that powered four electric tannoy speakers.

Disappearing slag heaps and a sinking boat

During my time at the island I was to see a tremendous change in the scenery ashore as land reclamation was in progress with the back-filling and landscaping of local opencast pits, and gradually the huge mountain-like slag heaps that had dominated the skyline of the surrounding area were all to disappear, leaving a gently undulating scene that blossomed green the following year. This region of Northumberland is now such a beautiful place that it is difficult to believe that its landscape was once an ugly and scarred industrial eyesore.

One of my predecessors at the station had made a small plywood rowing boat that was used for laying lobster pots in the deeper water offshore, or for fishing from, but a new use was found for it after Fred had been transferred. The new PK, weather permitting, would ask me to accompany him to row ashore to fetch the newspapers and fresh bread, when of course we took the opportunity to quench our thirst with a couple of pints of beer at the local pub. This all sounds idyllic, and to some extent it was, but one day we found the local kids had pinched our boat from the beach where we had left it, and were thrashing about in it in the harbour. It was only when we were part way back to the island, when water was sloshing around our feet, that we realised the boat had been damaged and was actually sinking around us. We had to swim the short remaining distance complete with bread, which thankfully was packed in plastic bags!

Throughout the Christmas of 1975 I continued to work despite having what I suspected was flu, but with the holiday over I finally reported sick and was brought ashore to see a local doctor whose diagnosis was that I did have flu, and I was immediately sent home on sick leave. During the period I was off work I had little idea that I would never return to the island, so it came as a complete surprise to learn that I was to be transferred to another station, which was to be South Stack at Anglesey. I had enjoyed my time at the Coquet despite its lack of facilities and the extra work involved in maintaining the old equipment and was sorry to leave it, but I was pleased to be moving on to something more up to date.

6

West coast

A lighthouse relief by taxi

On 10 February 1976 I reported to the Trinity House Depot at Holyhead to find that all my personal gear had arrived from the Coquet, and that unusually a complete change of crew was taking place at the Stack, three men on and three off, and that my two new colleagues were already at the lighthouse as

South Stack (Courtesy Chris Foulds)

they had arrived in Holyhead the day before, as was usual practice for those not living locally. As the South Stack was accessible from the shore the relief was carried out overland by taxi, so there would be no worries about delays due to weather.

With the taxi weighed down with stores and personal gear for all three men I made the ten-minute drive to the top of the cliffs at South Stack and discovered why the driver, with a wry smile, had said to me, 'you've never been here before, have you?' Situated on a small islet some 400 feet below us and approached by over 450 steps cut into the cliffside, and connected by a small footbridge was my new station.

My new PK was Calum Macpherson (Mac) who had travelled down from Seahouses near Berwick-on-Tweed in Northumbria, the other AK was Mark Hunter from Oxford, so I was very much the local boy.

The reason for the complete crew change was because the previous crew, who all lived locally in Holyhead, had allegedly been found missing from duty after the light was reported to be out by a passing vessel (probably one of the Irish ferries out of Holyhead). At a Board of Enquiry, instead of accepting a reprimand and transfer to an offshore station as punishment the men threatened to resign, whereupon, to their absolute astonishment and disbelief, this was accepted and they were all instantly out of work!

The interior of South Stack was such a contrast to that at the Coquet, it was much more modern, light and airy and had mains electricity with press button controls, running water (collected rainwater) for cooking and drinking purposes, supplemented by a rather brackish supply from a pond on Holyhead Mountain for

COLLECTING RAINWATER

In most cases rainwater was caught on the dwelling roof, ran down through downspouts and was stored in underground tanks. In cases where an explosive fog signal was in use, or in an area prone to heavy settlement of sea salt from spray, the roof had to be washed down by allowing the first hour of any appreciable rainfall to run away. Water from the tanks was pumped direct by a rotary hand pump into the dwelling ... it was not filtered or treated in any way. The tanks, just like fuel tanks, had to be cleaned regularly, which meant that after draining down a man had to climb in and bucket out the accumulated sludge. Likewise, the roof gutters and traps were cleaned regularly, and a close watch was kept for dead birds on the roof.

domestic use), a proper bathroom and an engine room the size of a ballroom and clean enough to eat in. We also had the luxury of a land-line telephone.

The lantern, 90 feet above the ground, contained a First Order lens weighing about two tons that floated in a trough of mercury, which when lit by its 3,000-watt lamp produced a light of 2,000,000 candle power making it sparkle like a crystal chandelier, unlike the badly chipped lens at Coquet. And with an electric motor drive replacing the clockwork mechanism, this was a very different proposition to the one I'd just left.

The fog signal was provided by 72 speakers in a separate detached building, but powered from their own alternators in the main engine room.

The area of South Stack is a place of outstanding natural beauty and as such is visited by many thousands of visitors each year, many of them making the rather dramatic descent down the cliff steps to visit the lighthouse where the keepers spent their days conducting group tours around the tower and lantern. The area is also noted for its high cliffs, which makes it a popular place for rock climbers. Each year there were incidents of climbers falling which required the services of the Coastguard Cliff Rescue team and helicopter, and since all these cliffs were visible from the lighthouse the keepers would invariably get the initial call from the rescue centre to confirm a reported incident (could we see the stranded or fallen climber), or we would be told directly of an incident by a member of the public or one of the other climbers and asked to raise the alert. So the keepers were a very important part of the community for this region.

Mermaid and helicopters

Because South Stack is such a wonderfully scenic place it was the location chosen by Roxy Music Records to photograph Jerry Hall, who was flown in specially from New York, as a mermaid for one of their LP covers, and I was there on the set as she posed on the rocks near the lighthouse. In the spring of 1978 Mac and I agreed to be interviewed at the lighthouse for Radio 4's *Down Your Way* programme; little did I know then that this was not going to be the only brush with radio and television companies that I would experience.

BARDSEY ISLAND

In October of that year, after being just one week on duty at South Stack I was instructed to go with the relief to Bardsey Island Lighthouse as Keeper-in-Charge as their PK had been taken ill, and as this was to be my first flight by helicopter since their introduction it was quite exciting. It had been intended that I should be at Bardsey for just one week but advised to take food supplies for ten days, but as events unfolded I remained there for four weeks, which resulted in short rations all round, and my spending time in hospital.

Bardsey is a small island of about 444 acres separated from the Lleyn Peninsula by the treacherous waters of Bardsey Sound; two miles long and half a mile wide, it is surrounded by outcrops of sharp rocks and fast swirling tides. In the sixth century this was a refuge for the Celts who were being persecuted by the Saxons, and St Dolmers, the patron of St Mary's Abbey, which had been built on the island, died here in 612. The bodies of many venerable monks were also conveyed to the island, and 20,000 saints are reputed to be buried here. The west

Bardsey Island

side of the island is quite flat and fertile, having once been used for agriculture to sustain a small farming community, while the east side is dominated by a steep mountain. The church of St Mary and many of the houses, at the time of my visit in various stages of dereliction are clustered near the northern end.

The lighthouse is built at the southerly tip and is a massive square red-banded tower rising to 99 feet. A First Order lens of five panels mounted on a mercury float carriage, combined with an electric light from diesel generators, provided a powerful 2,000,000 candle power light.

Two large dwellings stand within the lighthouse compound: the original keeper's two storey family dwelling attached to the tower, which is now used only for visiting personnel, and separated by a swathe of green lawn, a new dwelling for the regular relieving keepers. An engine room around the base of the tower and a separate fog signal stack complete the main buildings.

Situated on a migratory route, this light attracts many birds of all species. Many hundreds beat themselves to death on the windows each night, and in an attempt to reduce these fatalities the tower is floodlit.

ST BEES

The following year (1979) I was instructed to go on a holiday relief duty to St Bees in Cumbria, a shore-based station run two handed by one keeper and his wife. I had to go and relieve them both as it was usual practice to send only one man to cover the duty. St Bees Head Lighthouse is an attractive station that stands on the high clifftop at Sandwith just south of Whitehaven, and was until its modernisation in 1963 a family-run station. In 1822 it had burned to the ground with the tragic death of the keeper's wife and five children; the keeper himself survived and was found behind the main entrance door where the draught had sustained him. As a consequence of this all coal-fired lights were converted to oil, giving St Bees the dubious reputation of having been the last coal-fired lighthouse in the country. The modernisation in 1963 saw the introduction of mains electricity, resulting in a reduction of manpower from three keepers to just one keeper and his wife. A separate 30-tannoy speaker fog signal stack was built on the clifftop 150 yards away in front of the lighthouse.

St Bees Head (Courtesy Chris Foulds)

Risky cliff rescues

In January 1980, an event took place at South Stack that was to launch me into the newspaper headlines and interviews with many local radio stations in the northwest region … an event that would be referred to many times in the future.

During a quiet afternoon Mac and I were alerted by a couple of young boys coming to the lighthouse to say that their climbing instructor was injured, having fallen from the cliff below the lighthouse. Mac asked me to have a look while he alerted the coastguard. After climbing over the boundary wall I could see at the bottom of the cliff the injured man lying half in and half out of the water, and without thinking about it I climbed down the rock face to reach him (on reflection, and looking at the site later, I have no idea how I managed it). It was obvious from his screams that the injured man was in a lot of pain, and I suspected broken legs, and as we were in a rising tide it was necessary to get him out as soon as possible. I remained with the man, supporting him in the rising water until a cliff rescue team reached us, then with the injured man air-lifted out by helicopter I was unceremoniously dragged back up the cliff on the end of a rope. I had been in the water for approximately 45 minutes, and on a crisp January day, sea bathing in the Irish Sea is not recommended! After a change of clothes I was back on duty. I was to learn later that the injured man had actually broken his pelvis, and that after a stay in hospital he made a full recovery.

Two weeks later another incident occurred that required the assistance of the keepers, without whose presence the outcome could have been more serious than it was. On the opposite side of the island a group of adults were under instruction on rock climbing as part of an outward-bound course headed by one of the country's top ten climbers, John Cunningham. Having spent the best part of the afternoon climbing in a stiffening wind, one of the group fell into the sea and was swept away. One member with a rope around him jumped in to swim to his aid, but because the sea conditions were now rough the swimmer couldn't make any headway, and while trying to recover him, all but one of the remaining members of the party were swept off the rock. This sole survivor then came to the lighthouse for assistance, and once again a call was put out to the cliff rescue team. When Mac and I got down to the rocks we helped get bodies out of the water, but one man, the swimmer with the rope, was being hurled against the rock face by the heavy seas, and it took all our combined efforts to retrieve him. With darkness falling pretty fast, the rescue helicopter, using spotlights, managed to recover the first man from the water, and while the rescue team dealt with the more seriously injured on the rocks, I dealt with the minor ones at the lighthouse with the aid of the station's First Aid box. After the confusion of the incident it was discovered that one person was still missing, the instructor John Cunningham, and despite an extended search his body was never recovered. It was a sad and tragic episode. But it goes to show that, no matter how experienced you are, you should never be complacent or take things for granted, especially the sea.

The media gave the incident extensive coverage, and by some imaginative headlines many of the daily newspapers and television reports linked me with both rescues. In January 1981, to my astonishment and complete surprise, I was informed that I was to be awarded the Royal Humane Society Bronze Medal, 'For having saved the life of a citizen'. On the 26 February 1981, accompanied by my wife and two daughters I was presented with the medal at a special awards ceremony in my home town of Wigan at the Town Hall by the Mayor, Councillor Charles France, and the Deputy Chief Constable of Greater Manchester, John Stalker. I proudly wore the blue medal ribbon on my uniform for the rest of my service.

RHS bronze medal

Automation complete

Automation work within the lighthouse service was becoming a major talking-point, and work on various stations was well advanced, and in some cases complete. Even at this stage I think some men still doubted that automation was a viable prospect, as it had failed on previous attempts. Proof of that was here at South Stack because a scheme to operate Bardsey, North Stack, Skerries and South Stack via a VHF link had failed somewhat miserably, and all that redundant equipment was still here in situ. It was the automation of the Eddystone in May 1982 that really brought home to us that this new technology was working, and with the introduction of lantern-top helipads on the big rock towers giving all-weather access, we began to realise it was only a matter of time before it caught up with us all. The spring of 1983 brought a flurry of activity to the Stack with the arrival of engineers, and the delivery of equipment was an almost daily occurrence, and by late summer the lighthouse was actually operating automatically. The new equipment was simply grey nondescript metal boxes housing electrical circuits and microchips connected to the existing equipment and operated through a telephone or radio link to a nearby control point. Neatly fixed to the walls these boxes looked fairly innocuous at the time but were in fact to change the lives of many people. With automation now proving reliable within the Service, and with South Stack operating successfully it was time for the keepers to move on, and I was fortunate in being offered a posting to the Longstone Lighthouse at the Farne Islands in Northumberland, so after eight years and nine months at the South Stack I was to venture over to the east coast again.

7

East coast

The lighthouse of Grace Darling fame

The Farne Islands are situated some 50 miles north of Newcastle-upon-Tyne and have two lighthouses to give warning of their position. The Inner Farne Light marks the shoreward end, while the Longstone, standing on a tidal reef five

Longstone Light

Longstone switchboard

miles from the mainland, marks the outer or seaward end. I was joining the station as senior AK, and it was at the local harbour of Seahouses that I met up again with Mac, my ex-PK at South Stack who had transferred here a year previously. My second colleague was John Cooney who had served at Longstone for a number of years. Compared to the station I had just left, the Longstone could be called old fashioned as it was powered by single-cylinder Gardner L2 diesel engines producing 100 volts DC through an ancient open-knife switch-breaker board of the 1950s

Spectacle lens

that looked a nightmare, but proved to be quite simple to operate once I had got the hang of it. The lantern contained an unusual 'spectacle' lens mounted on a central pedestal, one of only two such lenses in the Service, with the main light being produced from two 1,000-watt lamps, one in each side of the lens, but despite having electrical power the lens was still rotated by a weight-driven clock mechanism. This was eventually to be the last hand-wound mechanism to be used in the service. Across a courtyard on the first floor of a separate accommodation block were the keepers' quarters where each man had his own bedroom. There was a bathroom, a separate radio room/office, a small kitchen with gas cooker, a living room with comfortable easy chairs and television, and an oil-fired central heating system, so we did at least have some comforts of home. The lower floor provided accommodation for visiting contractors or engineering personnel, storage space, and a radio beacon transmitter room. Rainwater from the roof was collected for domestic use, drinking water delivered by local boat, and sea water was used for the toilet.

The Longstone Lighthouse was made famous by the exploits of a young lady named Grace Darling, the daughter of the keeper William Darling, who in 1838

The rescue of the survivors of the Forfarshire *wreck is commemorated by this
wooden plaque on the wall of the room that was Grace Darling's bedroom
(Courtesy Chris Nicholson)*

went with her father, at great risk to themselves in the small lighthouse boat to a group of rocks about a mile away to rescue nine survivors of a shipwreck. Those survivors, after being brought to the safety of the lighthouse had to remain within the tower for a further two days before the weather was calm enough for rescue boats from the mainland to collect them. This, in Victorian days, was hailed as one of the greatest heroic deeds carried out by a young lady, and both she and her father were awarded gold medals by the rescue associations of the day. The story of Grace Darling is now part of our folk history and, as a result of her connection with the lighthouse, visitors touring the islands by boat were allowed to land, and the off-duty keepers spent their time conducting guided tours of the tower and relating the heroic tale.

Bombs, waterspouts and radiation

Another lesser-known event that brought the name of the station to the fore took place during the Second World War is commemorated on a plaque in the keepers' quarters: *These dwellings were erected in 1951 on the site of the former fog signal house which was destroyed by three bombs dropped on the diaphone tower by a German Heinkel aircraft, in the afternoon of Friday 1 August 1941.*

Apparently it was a fine afternoon and the three keepers were out on the rock when they heard the aircraft, and seeing the approaching attack they were able to take shelter behind the tower where they were safe from the blast.

At the end of 1983 the relief at Longstone was transferred from boat to helicopter, which should have made life a little better because the relief could be accomplished within 30 minutes, as opposed to one hour each way on the boat. However, as the North Sea lightships were at this time undergoing automation, the demands on the helicopter to fly men and materials out to them meant that our relief times were more often than not disrupted, and on many occasions it was to prove quicker and simpler to have the relief done by boat. Eventually it was the helicopter of the Scottish Lighthouse Service in Edinburgh that was used for the relief at Longstone and Coquet lighthouses, giving us a more reliable and quicker turnaround. Christmas 1983 saw me away from home on duty, but with regular dates throughout the year I was at home the following Christmas, and then after a routine year I was away again for 1985.

Many hobbies and pastimes were still practised at Longstone, and I made my first attempt at the much desired and traditional maritime undertaking of a ship in a bottle, but sadly, despite some really expert guidance from my colleague John Turney, an experienced modeller, I was to discover that my eyesight wasn't good enough for the fine detail work, so with disappointment I switched to larger models. In all I was to make from scratch three radio-controlled scale model boats. The first was a traditional Scottish puffer followed by a 1910 open-bridged coaster, both from wood, the third was a flat-bottomed car ferry made from tin plate that had once been the deep-freeze lid. When weather permitted, these boats were sailed on a tidal pond behind the lighthouse, and proved to be a great success.

It was here at the islands that I first saw the amazing spectacle of a developing waterspout, with not one, but two spouts reaching from the cloud base to water level, a quite spectacular event. As it passed at very close quarters I recorded the event in detail and submitted a short article about it to the Met Office, who eventually published it in their March 1986 Meteorological Society magazine more than a year after the event. I had seen these things in the past whilst at sea, when it was policy to give them a wide berth, but I had never seen one close up before; another wonderful experience.

Everyday things like water conservation and the collection of rainwater on lighthouses was second nature and so routine to keepers, that even after the news of the Chernobyl power station explosion in Russia in April 1986 it was some days before we realised the implications, and that due to contamination we could no longer collect rainwater for domestic use, which made life a little difficult until Trinity House made provision for water to be delivered.

A lighthouse on legs

In October 1986 I was promoted temporary PK and transferred to the Inner Dowsing Light Tower off the Lincolnshire coast. However, for some reason or other, I didn't actually get there until March the following year. Reporting for duty to the District Depot at Great Yarmouth I was bussed, along with the relief lightsmen from the North Sea lightvessels up to Cromer Lighthouse from where the helicopter would take us out to our various stations. The ID Tower was an ex-exploration drilling platform built for the National Coal Board in 1955 and sold to Trinity House in 1970 for conversion for use as a lighthouse. After conversion it was used to replace the Inner Dowsing lightvessel some 15 miles off the coast. Flying time to the tower was 30 minutes, and to see such a frail-looking object standing alone so far from land was not encouraging. Built of tubular steel sections the tower stood in 50 feet of water on a sandbank and had a flat top deck on which a helipad and lantern tower (ex-lightvessel) had been affixed. Wooden modules or cabins mounted beneath the working deck and helicopter platform provided the accommodation space, the centre of which was used as an engine room and power house.

Alongside Trinity House diesel generators were the original Crossley engines used to generate the huge amounts of power required to operate the drilling rig, but these were now far too large for the power requirements of the lighthouse and although still in situ, had been isolated. At that time the automation of about four lighthouses was being completed every year. I was therefore not surprised to find on my arrival the conversion of the Inner Dowsing station well under way. The new equipment was to be powered from a huge array of solar panels mounted on the upper deck for the main navigation light, racon (radar identification signal), fog signal, and anti-collision lights surrounding the platform.

Inner Dowsing tower

The original accommodation had been designed for approximately 25 men so there was more than enough space for the resident crew of engineers onboard as well as the keepers, unlike the situation I would encounter at other stations in later years. Before my duty period was finished the old light was decommissioned and the new system brought into operation, and after a period

FUEL TANKS

On mainland or island stations, a light mineral oil (LMO), a form of paraffin, was stored in a specially designated outbuilding, or on a separate floor in a tower. Storage tanks were circular or rectangular in shape and contained 100 and 200 gallons. Oil was delivered either by local boat in small containers, of say five gallons, or by ship, where sometimes it was possible to deliver the oil by transfer pump direct from a ship's launch at the landing into the tanks; at the Inner Dowsing Tower I saw it pumped direct by hose from the ship which anchored only a short distance from the tower.

Storage tanks had to be cleaned periodically, which meant one of the keepers entering the tank through the inspection hatch located at the top, and any remaining oil and residue at the bottom of the tank mopped out with cotton waste, placed into a bucket and hauled out above the keeper's head … not a pleasant job.

of running-in the engineers were happy for the station to become unmanned. So after I had been there for a single duty period the station was automated and all the keepers taken off. After my shore leave I requested, and was granted a return to Longstone, but to do so I had to revert to my old rank of Assistant Keeper. However, the consolation was that, owing to the temporary change of station when I had had to fall into a new system of relief dates, I would be home for the Christmas of 1987.

CAISSON LIGHTHOUSES

In 1880 German engineers designed a method of creating a stable foundation on which to build a lighthouse, or bridge support where the ground was soft or unstable. This entailed constructing on shore a vast iron tub or caisson; this was then towed out to sea to its selected site, and there sunk in the sand to form a solid base upon which to build. This huge tub was fitted with a vertical air shaft and formed the working place for the men who excavated the sand from the bottom of the sea. The whole case was made of boiler plate and above its bottom cutting edge, which would be forced into the sand by its own weight, was a steel floor which was used as a platform for mixing concrete. After the weight had caused the bottom edge to cut into the sand, the workmen climbed down to the bottom of the chamber onto the sandy sea bed and began to dig. The more sand was removed, the lower the huge tub would sink, its cutting edge digging further into the sea bed. When the correct depth had been reached concrete was poured into the bottom of the chamber to stabilise it, and when all was complete, a tower or bridge pier was erected on the upper deck.

TELESCOPIC LIGHTHOUSES

Lighthouses of various materials and design have been constructed to meet the requirements of local sea conditions and the type of ground that they have to be built on. Swedish lighthouse engineers invented the telescopic lighthouse. A giant concrete container was first constructed which served as the foundation and base of the lighthouse. A concrete tower was then built within the container. The whole thing could be built in the safety of a harbour and then floated and towed out to its allocated position at sea. Once on site the whole structure was sunk onto the sea bed (controlled sinking) and the inner part of the telescope then raised to form a tall sea tower upon which a light could be exhibited. The Royal Sovereign Light House off the coast of Kent is constructed in this manner.

Blue Peter *Badge*

In April 1988 I agreed to a BBC film crew from the televison programme *Blue Peter* coming out to Longstone to make a 'special' edition programme to celebrate the 150th anniversary of the rescue by Grace Darling in 1838, as the RNLI wanted to buy a new lifeboat for the local harbour and name her *Grace Darling*. The programme presenter was Mark Curry, and for assisting with the making of the programme I received my very own *Blue Peter* badge.

On 10 October, while on duty at Longstone, I received a telephone call from Trinity House offering me promotion to Principal Keeper at St Ann's Lighthouse in South Wales. After the initial shock and the realisation of what was happening within the Service I refused, because St Ann's was at that time still a family station. I would therefore be expected to take up residence, but with automation just around the corner, and my future in the Service so uncertain, I wasn't prepared at this late stage to give up my own home, or ask my wife to uproot and live there with me; so I remained a lowly assistant at Longstone.

I was at home for Christmas 1988, returning to work on 11 January 1989.

Alan Titchmarsh presents

On Tuesday 28 March 1989 Alan Titchmarsh, with a film crew from the BBC programme *Pebble Mill at One* arrived at Longstone to make a one-hour 'live' programme, and during the next couple of days the film crew (15 of them) arrived by boat each morning to set up their equipment, which proved to be quite considerable, and at the end of their working day went ashore to stay in a hotel. The day of the broadcast was glorious and sunny with clear blue skies, it couldn't have been better, and the lighthouse appeared beautifully on television.

Mac, myself and Ian McKintyre as keepers were to be interviewed by Alan in a live link-up with Judy Spears at the studio in Birmingham but, unbeknown to us was a featured item that came as a complete surprise to us all, especially Mac. Due to retire the following month, he was suddenly confronted by his daughter in the Birmingham studio who came on air to wish him a happy retirement and present him with a cake in the shape of the lighthouse, and Alan presented him with his Certificate of Service from Trinity House. Talk about being taken by surprise! After Mac's retirement I took over as temporary PK and applied for promotion under new regulations. Prior to these regulations promotion had traditionally been based on seniority within the Service (and I was next 'on turn' anyway), but now I had to apply, and if invited would have to go before a selection panel in London and prove my worth.

Shattered peace – promotion and obsolescence

At the beginning of May three contractors took up residence with us at the lighthouse to carry out preparatory work for the forthcoming automation, and our usually quiet and tranquil life was somewhat disrupted by early-morning and late-night noise. Throughout the spring and early summer the work continued, with different men staying for differing periods, all causing disruption to our routines and the operation of the lighthouse, and we were kept busy trying to keep on top of dust and dirt generated by them as well as do our own job.

In August 1989 I was summoned to Trinity House in London to appear before the promotion panel made up of Superintendents and senior managers, which was quite nerve-racking, but I met many of my colleagues there, some I'd not seen for many years, so in a way it was like a company reunion. On 11 September 1989 I was delighted to receive the news that I had been promoted to Principal Keeper and officially transferred to Longstone in that capacity. My crew members would be Paul Brodiak AK, John Cooney AK and Ian McKintyre AK.

The last of the hand-wound clocks

The automation work was gaining momentum. The old fog signal engines and their associated air tanks and pipework were all removed, new walls were built dividing the engine room into small fireproof units that would house continuous running diesel generators. Bricks and cement were everywhere and it was a nightmare trying to keep the light running with all the dust. Apart from those in residence at the lighthouse other engineers and contractors were coming and going daily as weather permitted, many of them overlapping with other tradesmen, and there was more than one incident where a little diplomacy was required to reach an amicable solution. After almost a year of disruption the official switch-over to automatic operation finally came on 6 June 1990, and on that day the hand-wound clock-work mechanism used to rotate the lens was finally discontinued, having been replaced by electric drive motors. The lighthouse was now running itself under automatic conditions and the keepers were in residence only in case of malfunc-tion or failure of the new equipment. There was little for us to do but maintain domestic services for our own labour force, who were still installing the security systems for the protection of the buildings after the last keeper left, so life was a little less hectic. The date for demanning was to be 26 September 1990, but sadly, as my final relief from the station was 12 September, I wasn't there at the end. After my leave I was to be transferred to a 'pool', whereby I would be avail-able for duty at any lighthouse for temporary relief duty, more or less as it was when I was training all those years ago, so what goes around comes around!

A pirates' hideaway

My first spell of 'pool' duty was to be at Lundy South Lighthouse, so off I went again, to Swansea where my career had begun, and to a station and island I was pleased to be returning to. I found many changes at the Trinity House Depot at King's Dock, and instead of boarding one of the tenders for this relief as would have been the case years previously, I was whisked away to Swansea airport for a flight by Trinity House helicopter. The flight time to Lundy was 25 minutes, and as the flight was over water all the way it wasn't the most interesting of flights, but that was to change as the island came into view. I was able to recognise landmarks and buildings I had known in the past. The approach to the island by air was a totally different experience than by sea, and before I knew it we were hovering over the landing pad at the South Light.

The changeover of men and their equipment was done very quickly below the rotating blades of the helicopter, and when entering the lighthouse I found that little had changed, many things being instantly recognisable and familiar despite the intervening years, which was comforting. The only addition to the station routine was that weather observations were recorded every three hours for the Met Office and coastguards, not my favourite pastime, but as I was only there for a short time I would learn to live with it. My colleagues here were Bob Collis PK, Chris Tye AK and Bob Farrah AK.

I always loved being at Lundy Island. During the summer months it can be reached by boat from either Ilfracombe or Bideford and the crossing takes about two hours. The west side of the island is exposed to the onslaught of heavy seas from the Atlantic Ocean while the east side faces the quieter waters of the

Lundy Island from the south

channel between it and the Welsh coast; the southern end faces Hartland Point in North Devon. At the south end of the island is a small village or settlement, complete with a massive church built by a Reverend Heaven, where the small community of inhabitants live and work. The island was bought from private hands in 1969 by the industrialist Jack Heywood and given to the nation in the care of the National Trust, who in turn lease it to the Landmark Trust. The Trust has invested heavily in restoration of all the properties and boat landing access, making it more comfortable and more accessible to visitors. There are two operational lighthouses on the island, one at each end, replacing a magnificent disused lighthouse on the highest point above the settlement. The island also has a hotel, manor house, a castle, and many other interesting buildings including its very own brewery. It also has an authenticated pirates' cave, as during the 18th century the island became the haunt of pirates for storing smuggled tea, brandy, gin and tobacco to evade the revenue men and tax duty.

I was looking forward very much to rediscovering some of the places of interest I had seen many years before, but my first surprise was that the island was not as flat as I had remembered, in fact it is quite undulating with the land rising uphill from The Three Quarter Wall to the north end. I did, however, remember how beautiful the brown and orange bracken looked, set between the green of the grass and the white outcrops of granite. A main track runs the length of the island and is marked by huge granite stones placed approximately

100 feet apart, positioned by quarry workers over 100 years ago. At the north end of the island towering stacks of weathered granite face the biting northerly winds, each stack appearing to be made of individual rocks stacked one upon the other and producing the most fantastic shapes. The North Lighthouse is situated on a plateau cut into the rock below the island rim, and is first seen through a crevice in the rocks which allows access to a long flight of rough-hewn steps. Since my previous visit 23 years earlier a fog signal stack had been added to the tower, but despite looking rust-streaked and abandoned the station looks much the same. It was quite strange entering the old place again after so many years. I remembered it as a dark and dismal place lit only by oil lamps, but now it was bright with electric light (available from a continuously running generator plant), and even a bathroom had been fitted.

I spent my time here enjoying the old sights, and realised just how relaxing the atmosphere and pace of life on the island were. While out walking one day I came across one of the residents who remembered me being on the island in the 1960s – there's fame for you! With my time on the island at an end, I was pleased to find that my relief by helicopter was to be on time. After the usual brief exchanges with the incoming keepers, my gear was loaded and I was soon in the air on my way to Swansea with the thought that I had enjoyed my first tour of duty as a 'pool' keeper.

I was informed whilst on leave, that in the new year I had a new permanent posting as Principal Keeper at the Needles Lighthouse in the Isle of Wight, but before taking up post there I would be required to go back to Lundy for another two weeks' pool duty with the next relief, so I was pleased about that.

My return visit to Lundy was on 10 December but, unlike my previous visit when I had been able to get out and about, I was confined to the lighthouse for some long spells by severe weather conditions. Nonetheless I did get some time out and enjoyed my stay there. On Sunday, 23 December the day before my relief, I was delighted to find that the weather had become settled and was fine and bright, good enough for me to walk up to the village to say my farewells to those I knew, but during the early hours of Christmas Eve morning a new weather front producing rain and 35-knot winds came through, so the prospect of a relief didn't look good. As the morning wore on the weather improved until we had a bright morning with only 15 knots of wind, and at breakfast I was delighted to learn that the helicopter was airborne and on its way. With little or no problems on the railways I made all my connections and arrived home at 6 p.m., so was home in time for Christmas in 1990.

8

Principal Keeper

The famous Needles Lighthouse

On 23 January 1991 I travelled by train via London Euston and Waterloo for a connection to Brockenhurst where I caught a local train that runs through the New Forest and connects with the Isle of Wight ferry at Lymington Harbour. I had never been to the Isle of Wight before and was interested to see the Solent and the approach to the island. During the crossing I could see in the distance the lighthouses at Hurst Point, and the Needles way down on the horizon, and I knew that come tomorrow the Needles would be a reality instead of just a picture postcard. At my overnight hotel I met my senior keeper Gerry Douglas-

Relief boat Maverick

Sherwood who was going out to the station with me, and as he had been at the Needles for something like ten years or more, I felt I was in good hands.

The Needles at this point was the last remaining lighthouse to have its relief carried out by boat, as all others were now done by helicopter. Because of the tide an early start had been arranged for the following morning, and at 5.50 a.m. sharp we were picked up by our boatman Tony Isaacs for the short journey to Yarmouth Harbour to board the relief boat, *Maverick*. At 6.10 a.m., after loading our supplies aboard, we set off in the darkness for the one-hour journey to the lighthouse. It was quite exhilarating to be sailing down the Solent on a calm clear morning before dawn, and as we turned south from the north-west corner of the island the bright red sector light of the Needles could be seen.

During the trip down Gerry told me that, despite the boat relief, overdues caused by weather conditions were a rarity here, and went on to explain the procedure about what would happen when we got to the lighthouse – who did what and in what order, etc., which was good to know because as the 'new boy' no one would be impressed if I got in the way of a perfected and regular safe routine.

On our approach to the light-house, with the sky beginning to brighten, the keepers could be seen assembling equipment on the landing. I could see that a helipad had been constructed over the roof of the tower, but apparently it hadn't been sanctioned for use, so until it was the boat relief was retained.

Needles Light

Boat relief (Courtesy Tessa Bunney)

Quite deftly Tony brought the boat's head up into the tide and kept it alongside the steps without the need for ropes, and after a quick greeting to everyone with our voices echoing in the stillness of the morning, we quickly unloaded the boat and exchanged the keepers. With the relief completed and the relieved men on their way home at an early hour it was time for introductions and the ubiquitous cup of tea. The third member of the crew, Paul Davies, was my junior keeper. He had already completed two weeks of his duty turn, so at the next relief in two weeks' time he would go ashore and another man would come onboard.

Needles Lighthouse stands at the western extremity of the Isle of Wight facing the Dorset coast and sits at the end of a set of chalk rocks that resemble giant sized dragon teeth. The 80-foot high tower has perpendicular sides and is of natural stone with a broad red band painted around its middle along with a red gallery and lantern. From the landing there are four semicircular steps up to a heavy gun metal entrance door that opens vertically in two halves. Inside the door a spiral staircase leads clockwise up to the left, and directly opposite the front door is the engine room, the first of six rooms. The diameter of all the rooms in the tower is approximately 12 feet, which means that space really is tight. Squeezed into this space in the engine room are four single-cylinder L2 Gardner engines and generators along with an open-knife breaker DC distribution switchboard.

This was a smaller version of that at Longstone, so I was pleased to see that I had an idea how to operate it.

The next floor up is a storeroom in which two domestic freezers, our individual food cupboards, and all station stores are kept. Above the storeroom comes the heart of the lighthouse, the kitchen, and what a surprise this turned out to be! A room only 12 feet across with three windows, built-in base and wall kitchen units, a sink unit, a gas cooker and a solid-fuel cooking range arranged around two-thirds of the room, and in the centre a table with three cottage-style easy chairs. This room also contained the television, two ship-to-shore radios, the telephone, weather recording instruments and the station log books, so it was apparent that this was where most activities took place.

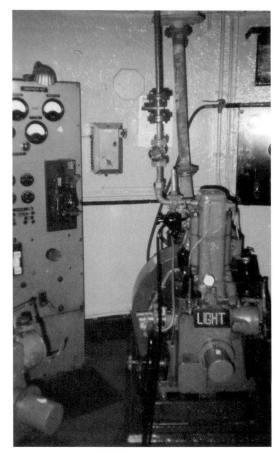

Lighting engine

On the floor above is the bedroom, a communal room with five curtained bunks in two tiers built around the wall, along with two standard upright wardrobes. The centre space of the room was not utilised, making the room appear quite large, and because of the keepers' shift patterns this was simply a room for sleeping. Two windows gave light and air, and despite the room's location high up in the tower, it was occasionally necessary to bolt the windows down because of high seas. Going up one more floor to the fifth room was the service room, a room where, in years gone by, the duty keeper maintained his watch throughout the night, being in close proximity to the oil lamp above in the lantern. As our power was generated on the ground floor it was now more convenient for the keeper to be available near the bottom of the tower. The room also contained a built-in curved cabinet where spares for the lamps were once kept, a flush toilet (a loo with a view!), a shower cubicle (powered by battery) and two domestic fridges for everyday use (two floors up from the kitchen!). Above this room was the lantern, the working end of the lighthouse so to speak, the light being produced from a 1,000-watt electric lamp inside a fixed lens that was elevated on a sub-gallery floor at window level. The light is seen from various angles as mainly white, but it also has red and green sectors. The space below the lens and known as the lower service room contains the main light switch gear and two air compressors, air tanks and associated equipment to operate a fog signal. An external door gives access to the outer gallery where the foghorn trumpets are located, and a fixed ladder leads to the newly-erected helipad above the lantern roof.

The storage of fuel, coal and gas was not inside the tower but in a cave cut into the chalk cliff at the back of the landing, and because of its location it was always important to be aware of the fuel situation as well as the weather forecast, as it was not uncommon to have heavy seas breaking over the landing for days on end, making it impossible to get to the cave.

As described earlier, the keepers of lighthouses spent their spare time in many ways, and in the past I had done model making, cross stitch and fishing, etc. I had also been heavily involved with tourists in several places, but here at Needles, because of the confinement of the tower, I was to take up something entirely different. My colleague Gerry was a founder member of the Association of Lighthouse Keepers (ALK), an association aimed at keeping the history and heritage of the Lighthouse Service and the keepers alive after the automation and demanning of the Service. He was also the editor of its quarterly newsletter *Lamp*, articles for which he thumped out on a portable typewriter on the kitchen table, and as one of the traditional pastimes of keepers was storytelling, Gerry would say to me after I had told him some tale or other, 'write it down before you forget it'. He encouraged me to begin writing, much of which, to my surprise, he considered suitable for publication.

Looking back at my first year at Needles I have to admit I had a great time there, I had good colleagues who were good company and totally reliable, but for a lighthouse where overdue reliefs were a rarity, 1991 proved itself as six of them were late, five of them by as much as 24 hours.

Lighthouse Control Centre

My relief for returning to work after the Christmas of 1991, for which I was at home, fell on Boxing Day. With no public transport available that day enabling me to travel, I was instructed to report for temporary duty at Holyhead Lighthouse Control Centre on 1 January instead, and return to Needles to pick up my regular turn at the mid-term relief on 9 January. I had not been to Holyhead Depot since leaving South Stack in 1983 on transfer to Longstone, and with the automation programme progressing this was an opportunity to see and experience what went on in one of the new Lighthouse Control Centres being established around the country. It was envisaged that there would be about ten of these control centres in strategic positions, each monitoring the lights within a given area or district, and some lighthouses had already been adapted for this new role. The ex-depot building at Holyhead was at this time the largest purpose-built facility using this new technology, and a centre that was expected to grow as more and more automatic lights were routed to it in the future. The depot of old had undergone a radical change, as instead of a servicing depot it was now a residential centre operated by lighthouse keepers for the monitoring of the automatic west coast lighthouses, staffed by five keepers and one civil driver/labourer. Although initially drawn from those who lived in and around Anglesey, travelling from their homes for duty as required, this proved to be impracticable in the long term because the men from outside the area who were required to cover for absences needed living accommodation. The building was therefore converted to residential accommodation so that those on duty were on hand.

The control centre monitored all the electrical systems of each automated station round the clock via telemetry links to a computer, and operated by remote control their diesel engines, fog signals and secondary standby systems if required. The men also made regular visits to some of the stations by either road or boat for routine first line-maintenance (or investigation in the event of a breakdown), and husbandry duties. Although I didn't become a computer 'whiz kid' during my short stay, I did get to see the changing role of the traditional lighthouse keeper, and the new face of lighthouse keeping.

The stations monitored by the Holyhead Control Centre at that time were:

Souter Point (Tyneside), Radio Beacons
St Bees Lighthouse, Cumbria
Trwyn-Du Lighthouse, Penmon, Anglesey
South Stack Lighthouse
St Tudwal's Island Lighthouse
North Stack Fog Signal Station (disc. 1987)
Mersey Bar Lanby (Large Auto Navigation Buoy)
Point Lynas Lighthouse, Anglesey
Bardsey Island Lighthouse
Skerries Lighthouse

My return to Needles on the first relief of the new year on 9 January 1992 was to rekindle memories of past boat reliefs. In an attempt to get the men who had been on duty over Christmas relieved and away home, I and my colleague, as the on-going crew, agreed that although under normal circumstances we wouldn't attempt a relief because of the rough seas, we would sail down to the lighthouse and do our best to transfer from *Maverick* by rubber dinghy. With *Maverick* lying as close to the lighthouse as possible we transferred, with some difficulty, ourselves and stores from the large boat to the dinghy, then a short bumpy ride over the intervening distance brought us to the landing area. From a dinghy bouncing off the wall, and trying to do somersaults, it took a great deal of effort in a dangerous situation to balance and pass up heavy food boxes, so there was little time for chat and a quick turnaround was achieved. Although cold and wet we were pleased to have been able to relieve our colleagues who were now on their way home at an early hour. In the warmth of the tower over a nice hot cup of tea tales of other hair-raising reliefs were related, and it was with hindsight that we realised that what we had just done had been a calculated and dangerous thing, but it had paid off. However, had the off-going men not spent Christmas onboard a relief would not even have been attempted.

The Solent, apart from being a main route for cargo ships, ferries and cruise ships heading for Southampton, has been described as Britain's busiest leisure seaway, and as such there were always small boats to be seen. Throughout the summer it was inevitable that casualties would occur, and at the request of the coastguard the keepers at the Needles sometimes spent many hours watching over the area, or perhaps just monitoring one particular incident after receiving a distress call. So there was plenty to keep us occupied beside our own duties. It was not all doom and gloom here, as I was on occasion privileged to witness the triumphant return home of some famous yachtsmen and the sleek round-the-world yachts, solo and multi-crewed. Seeing them under full sail with their decks lined with crew members and the assembled flotilla of the welcome committee and press boats was quite a sight. On occasion we were privileged to be able to talk to these yachtsmen by radio to welcome them home.

With the automation of the offshore lighthouses progressing well, attention was turned to removing families from the remaining land-based lighthouses with a view to double-manning them on a relieving basis the same as rock stations. This would preserve jobs in the short term, so there was a certain amount of upheaval and transfer of personnel taking place. Some men would only be in post for a short time before redundancy, others would be moved from one station to another as each one demanded, but the overall effect was a diminishing workforce.

Early in the summer of 1992 the helipad at Needles was commissioned, and as I would now be flying on a regular basis I was sent on a helicopter crash survival course which involved having to escape from a 'dunker', a mock helicopter that is immersed in water and then revolved, the occupants having to leave it safely underwater; another interesting experience. For one reason or another only periodic reliefs by helicopter took place during the year, and we had to revert to the well-known boat method, and so it was for the Christmas relief that in good weather and sea conditions the relief was done by boat on time on 23 December; another year I was at home in time for Christmas.

Television fame with Blind Date

With regional television companies reporting the demanning or closure of their local lighthouse, the media in general was showing an ever increasing interest and I did many interviews with press, radio and television companies about the demanning of the station and the forthcoming end of a manned lighthouse service. I also participated in Cilla Black's programme *Blind Date*, the popular television show where two young people of the opposite sex are matched together and sent on a weekend date which is filmed and shown on the programme the following week. But I hasten to add that my part in it was not as a contestant. It was to show the winning contestants from the previous week around the lighthouse when, with a film crew in tow, they spent a day with us as part of their prize. Having been given the 'grand tour', the couple were filmed performing a couple of menial tasks in the lantern before climbing onto the rooftop helipad where some quite stunning scenes were filmed.

One of the Isle of Wight's claims is that it has a needle that can't be threaded! Well have I got news for you, that is no longer true, since in July 1993 contractors drilled a hole through one of the chalk needles directly behind the lighthouse so that an underwater electric cable from the main island could be laid to provide power to the lighthouse, enabling automatic equipment to operate. In September the same year, press and television companies crowded into boats to witness the famous needles being 'threaded' when the cable was raised from the sea bed and fed through the hole to provide a connection point in our store cave, thereby showing that the Needles had been threaded after all! (16 September 1993). The connection of mains electricity would bring about the discontinuance of the present diesel generators, when the tower would revert to its former quietness.

With preparation work for automation being contracted to outside companies it was a bit of a novelty having men unfamiliar with the Service staying on station, but space was always a problem. Despite sharing our limited accommodation with them there initially reigned a tolerance of each other that on the whole worked well. There were, however, the selfish few who created problems with the simplest of things like cooking and dish washing, and who, unused to confined living, treated our space as a hotel, which inevitably led to friction. The workload of the keepers was also increased because it was necessary every day or so to take on extra water supplies delivered by boat.

With heightened interest from the media there were plenty of distractions when we entertained journalists on station for a couple of hours, and some memorable interviews took place with well-known journalists and regional television reporters. One notable personality was Michael Palin, who spent a day with us. What never ceased to amaze me, though, was that these film crews would come out to the lighthouse to film about how isolated it was, and how keepers lived in cramped basic conditions with few luxuries, and yet it never crossed the mind of any of them to bring out the simplest of things like a newspaper, and sadly the promise of a video of the interview or finished programme was seldom kept. One of the better documentary programmes to be made was filmed over a period of three days for the BBC's *Open Space* programme and entitled *Lighthouse Keepers* in which all three keepers participated; and I am pleased to say that on this occasion copies of the programme were received.

Michael and I at Needles

In October 1993 my wife and I were returning home from New York aboard the *QE2*. Having come to the end of a most memorable holiday and thinking it couldn't have been any better there was, unbeknown to us, a fantastic finale, and one we shall never forget. At 11 a.m., as we entered the Solent opposite the Needles for our run-up to Southampton, a welcome home message radioed to the ship from my colleagues at the lighthouse was broadcast over the ship's open-deck speakers for all to hear. With the light flashing, foghorn sounding, and keepers waving from the rooftop helipad, this was a welcome home that could never be forgotten, especially as our ship responded with four long blasts on its whistles. Wow! ... how do you beat that!

Welcome home from colleagues

A visit by Father Christmas

Throughout life it seems that Christmas is the landmark that almost always takes us by surprise, and before you know it, it's there again. Having been home for Christmas for the past five consecutive years I couldn't complain to find that I was to be on duty during the Christmas of 1993, and I travelled to the Isle of Wight on 22 December. In fairly heavy seas, with little prospect of a possible relief, the boat buffeted its way down the Solent to the Needles, but on arrival the size of the sea swell meant it wasn't possible to get the big boat alongside. By mutual agreement we once again opted to attempt a risky transfer by rubber dinghy, a venture that provided a hair-raising ride and an extremely difficult landing, but we managed it. Transferring heavy food boxes from a lurching rubber boat is certainly not recommended, but without any undue incident or injury we managed it, and much to the delight of our colleagues they were off home for Christmas.

Christmas time at Needles was always a bit special as it was the only station I served at that received a visit from Father Christmas, who came out to deliver a food hamper. It was traditional here for Father Christmas to come out aboard the lifeboat from Yarmouth accompanied, weather permitting, by a flotilla of small boats and members of the Cowes Yacht Club who each year donated a Christmas hamper and tree to the keepers.

The lifeboat would stop some distance from the lighthouse and fire a rocket line which the keepers retrieved and then hauled in to set up a breeches buoy on which the tree and packages were transferred. The whole occasion was usually one of great fun for all concerned, even in foul weather, and the yachtsmen enjoyed the spectacle of the transfer, and we knew we were receiving a generous gift. At the end of the proceedings, with waves from Father Christmas, the boats celebrated by blowing their horns and whistles in a cacophony that could no doubt be heard for miles around. And when it was all over, in the warmth of the kitchen by the glow of the fire we put up the tree and unpacked this most welcome gift, amazed and thankful for the generosity of those involved. We had known before going on leave in November that this would be the last Christmas that the Needles was to be manned so we intended to make the best of it, and like other Christmases

I had spent on duty, it was a cheery occasion. The tree was decorated and cards and streamers put up, and Christmas Day, just as at home, was very special when presents and cards from home were opened, and all three men contributed to the cooking. After a traditional Christmas dinner, including the plum duff and a few drinks, we sat around the table in paper hats to think of family and friends and reminisce of past Christmases on other stations.

Although lighthouses were officially 'dry' it was usual to treat ourselves to a couple of nice bottles of wine at Christmas, and the hamper delivered by Father Christmas invariably had a bottle or two as well, so we were well provided for. However, the men were always aware that they had an important job to do, so things didn't get out of hand.

The year 1994 brought a flurry of activity aboard the station when our already cramped quarters were put under further pressure with the arrival of more contractors and engineers, and although I understood the need for these men to be there, after six months the novelty of having them onboard was wearing pretty thin. Tool boxes, drills and cables filled our very limited space for days and weeks on end, and it was astonishing how much noise, debris and dust were created drilling through the thick granite floors and walls. As the regular keepers were still required to work through the night I was constantly having to ask that working areas be left clear at the end of the working day to prevent accidents with abandoned equipment. A further request for a couple of hours of reasonable quietness during the day for the overnight watchmen to catch up on sleep at times created an air of tension. On the departure of these men there was always a great sigh of relief that we had our own space back, even if it was only for a few days.

9

The changing face of lighthouse keeping

Having been headhunted by the crew of Holyhead Control Centre I had applied for a transfer there which, to my delight was granted, and I finally left Needles by boat on 8 August 1994 prior to its demanning.

Holyhead Lighthouse Control Centre

On arrival at Holyhead I was to work under the instruction of the retiring PK Bill O'Brien who was in his last month of duty, and who would show me the duties of the control centre. For my first week Bill was very patient, explaining the procedures for monitoring and controlling the twelve out-stations via their telemetry and computer links, and the scheduled tasks to be carried out when visiting the automated out-stations. These were visited by either road or contract boat hire to carry out first-line maintenance and routine husbandry duties, so there was a lot to take in. After Bill's retirement my crew would be: Steve Davies AK, Chris Foulds AK, Peter Halil AK, Peter Riches AK and Gerry McKenna AK, and a civilian driver/labourer, Colin Brown. I had worked with Steve, Chris, Gerry and Pete Riches before so knew them to be conscientious and reliable workers, and Colin proved to be indispensable, his remarkable knowledge of all the out-stations was invaluable.

During my second week I accompanied the Marine Superintendent, Capt. Catesby, on a tour of inspection of the district when he wanted to visit all six out-stations. This was an ideal opportunity to see the stations' standby and auxiliary systems in operation as they were tested manually, which was valuable experience. The first visit was by road to Point Lynas, a castellated fortress of a place built and operated initially by the Liverpool Dock Board in 1835. A flight by helicopter on the second day took us to the islands of Skerries, St Tudwal's and Bardsey, so a full day indeed, but a thoroughly good grounding of future requirements in my new position. On the third day the inspection was of my old station South Stack, and despite the years since my last visit it seemed like only yesterday that I'd been running up and down those cliffside steps. The station was now automatic and had no public access, and the gulls seemed to think it was a heaven-sent undisturbed roosting place. Their droppings covered the roof, walls and yard area – a far cry from the pristine place it once was – and the abandoned interiors were eerily quiet, their bareness accentuated by the lack of personal possessions. At the end of the day the tour of inspection was declared a success and the entire crew received their accolades in writing. The Superintendent went away happy in the knowledge that the stations along the west coast soon to be under my care were in safe and capable hands.

The following are the automated stations along the west coast monitored by Holyhead Lighthouse Control Centre in 1994/5:

*St Bees Lighthouse, Cumbria
(Courtesy Chris Foulds)*

Local attendant.
Mains electric.

Trwyn-Du Lighthouse, Penmon, Anglesey

Accessed by road and causeway at low
water or by our own rubber dinghy.
Acetylene gas.

Bar Light Float, River Mersey

Trinity House tender.
Onboard diesel generators.

Point Lynas Lighthouse,
Anglesey

By road.
Mains electric.

Skerries Lighthouse

Contract boat from Holyhead.
Boatman Reg Biddlecombe.
Diesel generators.

Out-station status
information board.

South Stack Lighthouse

By road ... Cliffside steps and
footbridge.
Mains electric.

Bardsey Island Lighthouse

By road then contract boat
from Aberdaron.
Boatman Ernest Evans.
Diesel generators

St Tudwal's Island Lighthouse

By road then contract boat from
Abersoch.
Boatman Merion Lloyd Jones.
Acetylene gas.

*Lynmouth Foreland Lighthouse,
N. Devon (Courtesy Chris Foulds)*

Local attendant.
Mains electric.

Lundy Island South Light

Local attendant.
Diesel generators.

Author at work

Mumbles Head
(Courtesy Trinity House Collection)

Local attendant.
Solar power.

Not being tied to a single lighthouse and having available transport meant that we had the freedom to roam throughout the region doing whatever was required to maintain the lights of the area. It also meant that if required we were available to do various jobs for the Swansea-based maintenance department when on routine visits to the out-stations. As my new position now included a greater involvement with helicopters, I attended a helicopter marshalling course whereby I was taught how to give the pilot visual instructions in moving the helicopter up, down, left, right, forward, backward, and the precision lifting and placing of underslung loads, a seriously responsible job that needed full concentration.

The end of the gas era

Over the following year, one of two remaining gas-operated lighthouses in the care of the control centre that required a frequent presence during its conversion to automatic operation was Trwyn-Du. This stands on a small group of tidal rocks at Penmon at the north end of the Menai Straits; it has a black-and-white striped tower with a series of metal dog steps set into the masonry leading to the access door 30 feet above the base. Entering the lighthouse was like stepping into a time warp, something from the past and yet totally functional. The small circular living room with its blackleaded ornate iron fireplace, slopstone sink and water pump, and the now empty bedroom have all remained untouched since the last keeper left in 1921. There had never been any electronic monitoring of the station in the past, as the light set high above in the lantern was powered by acetylene gas that operated with minimum maintenance from a light intensity valve. The control centre relied on a nearby resident to keep an eye on the light and let us know if it wasn't lit, otherwise we assumed it was operating. Refuelling of the station was done by the crew of THL *Farne*, a small Trinity House launch. The crew would either carry or drag the heavy acetylene bottles over the rocks to the lighthouse at dead low water, or deliver them by launch when the tide was full,

DALEN GAS LIGHT

In 1906 Gustav Dalen developed a reliable and cheap automatic gas burner, making it possible for lighthouses (and buoys) to be unattended. A mixture of dissolved acetylene gas and air passed through a mixer and regulator to emerge at a burner head, producing a light that was able to operate for 12 months without attendance. Combustion of the mixture resulted in a hot, non-luminous flame which caused a mantle to become incandescent, and the pulsing action of the mixer was used to drive the optic pedestal at a predetermined speed. A small pilot light remained lit during the day, and from this the main burner was ignited when required by the control of a sun-valve. As the light could be left unattended for long periods, it was necessary to provide against mantle failure caused by damage. This was achieved by an ingenious device which, when a mantle was damaged, allowed the unconfined flame to burn through a wooden retaining peg, which in turn released a new mantle from clockwork-operated magazine and brought it into position above the burner nozzle. Dalen was awarded the Nobel prize for physics in 1912, and although refinements were made to it, his burner remained basically unchanged and was to continue in use until 1995.

tying up directly to the lighthouse tower. Either way, the presence of the control centre staff to assist was always necessary. Occasionally it was more convenient for us to board the launch at Menai and sail round with her to the station, which in fine weather was always a good day out. The upgrading of this station was to solar power, the solar panels required for charging banks of batteries being fitted to the gallery outside the lantern, and an uninspiring collection of grey plastic boxes containing electrical circuit boards, microchips and telemetry system was installed, the gas burner in the lantern being replaced by low-voltage bulbs.

TH helicopter (Courtesy Chris Foulds)

The second of the two gas stations where work was about to begin on upgrading was St Tudwal's, another station that had been unattended for many years but now required a complete makeover. As the station was in the care of the control centre it was visited regularly for routine maintenance and refuelling, but part of our task now was to assist with the delivery of building materials and equipment to the island. Putting my new skills in helicopter control to the test, I and some of my crew went down to the island to assist in the delivery of many tons of material. I spent ten hours on the small island giving the pilot directions in the placing of underslung loads into designated places, and with over 100 helicopter lifts in a day it was a mammoth task.

Sitting on the highest point of St Tudwal's Island, the lighthouse bearing this name has a very short tower and stands adjacent to a flat-roofed dwelling, now derelict, that was once the home for the two resident keepers and their families. Like many of the small island lights around our coasts, in 1922 it was fitted with an automatic acetylene gas light allowing the station to become unmanned, and like Trwyn-Du it was now being converted to solar power, both stations having a similar lighting system from low-voltage bulbs.

The 1990s was a period of rapid change within the Service with each year bringing a clutch of new automated stations on line along with the ultimate redundancies. With the regional control centres looking like the way ahead we thought that our days of being confined to a tower out at sea were over, but little did we know what lay in store for us.

Entering the computer age

Early in January 1995 my contentment with this new type of working was shattered. By the first post of the year I received official notification from Trinity House that as new technology could now give greater flexibility and greater range for control of automated stations, the Holyhead Control Centre was to close. All its monitoring functions were to be transferred to a single Operations Control Centre based at the main depot at Harwich and local husbandry tasks now undertaken by us were to be done by locally recruited attendants or caretakers. It was envisaged that by March that year the manning level at Holyhead would be cut to just one Principal Keeper and one Assistant Keeper on each watch, and all our operations transferred by August. This was totally unexpected and came right out of the blue, and it was with great disappointment that I saw my crew dispersed or made redundant. These sudden changes in policy were very disturbing, as any long-term future within the Service I thought I might have now seemed somewhat uncertain. As one of the remaining senior keepers I immediately requested a transfer to North Foreland after the closure of the control centre. This was one of the few remaining manned lighthouses where I knew there was a vacancy for a Principal Keeper.

After the monitoring equipment and computers had been removed from Holyhead there was little left for the remaining men to do but oversee the removal and disposal of the fittings and keep the building secure. With time to reflect on the closure and the disappointment of not having the long-term appointment that I'd hoped for, I at least had the good fortune of having been accepted for the vacant post of PK at North Foreland. For the time being my short-term future seemed assured. My final duty in association with the control centre came with the annual inspection of the area's lights by a Visiting Committee of Elder Brethren

THV Patricia (Courtesy Alan Nicholas)

when my colleague and I spent a full day with them aboard the Trinity House flagship *Patricia* on what was to be their last accompanied tour of inspection of our out-stations. All were impressed by the new installations and the reliability of the equipment and offered solace for the disappearing role of the lighthouse keeper.

I eventually left Holyhead on 4 July, and on 2 August 1995, Trinity House closed down its operation there after 120 years, cutting its links with the town.

Another new regulation recently imposed on the workforce was the requirement to become self-relieving. Instead of Trinity House maintaining its 'pool' of spare keepers to cover for absences, the existing workforce would have to provide cover themselves. As our working agreement had always been for 'time on' and 'time off', for the men to now have to give up a fortnight of their annual leave was not only very unpopular but a retrograde step in employment relations. Before taking up my appointment at North Foreland in August 1995 I was obliged under these regulations to carry out a relief duty at Flamborough Lighthouse in Yorkshire. Although I initially considered this to be an imposition, it was in fact a pleasant distraction as it gave me the opportunity to visit a station I had heard so much about but had never visited before.

Flamborough Head

My encounter with satellites

North Foreland, standing in the suburbs of Broadstairs, had until fairly recently been manned by resident keepers and their families, but as part of the current automation programme the families had been removed and the station converted into a regional control centre. This was manned by relieving crews that monitored the automatic lights around the Dover Straits and the notorious Goodwin Sands – Varne, North Goodwin, Falls and Tongue lightvessels – and three large buoys: Galloper, F3 and Greenwich, plus one automatic lighthouse: Beachy Head. However, by the time of my appointment, the monitoring of all but Beachy Head had been transferred to Harwich Central Control. As the station was shore-based, the relief here was carried out by taxi so there was never any delay when changing crews.

The site of North Foreland holds a strategic position on the Kent coast, being the waymark for vessels entering the Thames from the Dover Straits and the Southern North Sea. It can also lay claim to 500 years of continuous lighthouse

North Foreland

keeping as a coal light was first exhibited here in 1499, with the present tower dating back to 1692.

The octagonal tower is flanked by two cottages and surrounded by vast lawns (almost one acre), with an approach down a wide tree-lined driveway. The adjacent property to the lighthouse is a convent and some of the nuns, along with other neighbours, were to become regular and welcome visitors to the lighthouse.

The lantern provides a warning light from a 3,500-watt lamp protected by a 500-watt battery standby lamp inside a First Order static lens. There is no fog signal at this station, but a radio beacon, and for the first time I came across

Lens and lamps at North Foreland

a Differential Global Positioning System (DGPS). The familiar GPS service is nowadays considered to be the primary navigation aid, not only for shipping but for all types of travellers including ramblers, yachtsmen, canoeists, the emergency services, and for in-car navigation. This service is provided by a series of 24 satellites (owned and maintained by the American military) that circle the earth transmitting positional information, and with the appropriate receiving equipment a position to within 5–10 metres can be obtained, which is considered sufficient for general navigation purposes. DGPS, however, is in effect GPS with corrections, a service whereby the natural errors and certain built-in protective systems of the GPS system are corrected to give an accuracy of 2–3 metres. This information is then re-transmitted over a 50-mile radius and is available for specialised operations such as the positioning of oil rigs or cable laying. A computer at North Foreland downloaded the GPS data, calculated and applied the corrections and the new information was then transmitted. I had now reached the point of having gone from oil light to satellites in my career with Trinity House.

10

The final act

With the last of the stations undergoing automation, the end of a manned lighthouse service moved closer and redundancies were a common occurrence as each station came on-line. The keepers from those stations were pre-warned of either an approximate date for release or transfer to another station, and this meant that at North Foreland there was to be a constant stream of replacement third and fourth keepers as the junior men were released, and then finally the information we had all been waiting for was declared. North Foreland was officially designated as the last lighthouse to be demanned. No date for its demanning was given at that point, but with stations still undergoing conversion, for the time being I found myself Principal Keeper of what was to be Britain's last manned lighthouse.

A public farewell

Now that the lighthouse held the distinction of being 'Britain's last manned lighthouse', and as it wasn't generally open to the public, I requested and was given permission by Trinity House to hold an 'open week' whereby the local residents could come along and see the place before the keepers left. A small artefact exhibition and a picture gallery consisting of our own lighthouse collections was set up in the entrance of the tower, which proved to be a popular draw and gathering point for our visitors. The main topic of concern from our neighbours was the future, not only of the men, but also of the buildings. The local press and radio stations gave us good coverage, and I was pleased to find that many local people took the time to ring in to say how much they appreciated the opportunity, or that they had enjoyed their visit. In fact the week proved to

St Ann's Head (Courtesy Chris Foulds)

be so popular that because of sheer numbers we kept it going for another week, disassembling it on the last Sunday before the changeover relief was due.

In November 1996 I was once again seconded for standby relief duty, this time I was to go direct from North Foreland to St Ann's Lighthouse at the end of my duty, so instead of going home on leave I travelled across country to Haverfordwest in South Wales for a fortnight. After only two weeks' home leave I was away again on 10 December on what was to be the Christmas relief at North Foreland, so it was Christmas away from home in 1996.

Lizard Lighthouse

There were many rumours and counter rumours about the date of the end of the Lighthouse Service, and comings and goings of personnel owing to redundancies. To my annoyance that in July 1997 I was instructed to travel to Cornwall directly from North Foreland at the end of my duty period for two weeks' standby duty at Lizard Lighthouse. This extra duty covering for absences was becoming a bone of contention as there were men leaving the Service hand over fist, and the time we were having to cover was increasing.

It was with some relief that after another year of uncertainty the date for the demanning of North Foreland was announced as 26 November 1998, and with the forthcoming Christmas being the last one any keeper would be away from home, it gave us the opportunity to reflect on all the past Christmases spent away from home and families. I was fortunate that for this final Christmas I would be at home, and I travelled home without undue incident on 10 December 1997 in the sure knowledge that I wouldn't ever have to spend another Christmas away. After so many years that was actually a strange feeling.

LIGHTHOUSE POSTAGE STAMPS

In the spring of 1998, the Royal Mail proposed issuing a set of 'lighthouse' commemorative stamps. I agreed to partici-pate in publicity pictures for their launch in the south-eastern region. A day spent with a photographer at the lighthouse result-ed in the pictures that were released to the press for advertising the stamps, and stamp posters that were displayed in all post offic-es throughout the region.

The last of the Welsh lighthouses

The preparations for automation at North Foreland were ongoing throughout the spring of 1998, the innocuous-looking boxes of microchips and printed circuits being fitted giving no clue to the changes that would finally see the end of the traditional lighthouse keeper.

Publicity pictures for lighthouse stamps

Complacent in the knowledge that as a senior keeper I would continue to be employed for the best part of the coming year, and perhaps right up to the closure date, I was staggered when I received six months' notice of redundancy. My last day of service was given as 15 September 1998, and I was deeply disappointed to find that with effect from the end of April I was to be transferred to Nash Point Lighthouse in South Wales. This meant that the two senior men above me would be on duty at North Foreland on the final day. As Nash Point was the last manned lighthouse in Wales it required a senior keeper to be there, and I had been nominated. On reflection I suppose I should at that stage have been grateful to be going to another lighthouse at all and not being made redundant.

After a period of sick leave I reported for duty at Nash Point on 10 June, and found that although the station had a full complement of keepers, its operational side was actually in the hands of the engineering department and still in the process of being automated. The tower was a complete shambles, the whole of the interior plasterwork, from top to bottom, had been hacked off, and cables sprouted from newly-installed control boxes like tendrils on an uncontrolled vine. My crew members here were Colin Bale AK, and Barry Simmonds AK, and apart from maintaining security and keeping an eye on a temporary battery-powered light each night, there was virtually very little else for us to do but keep the dust and dirt under control and cut the grass.

Nash Point, once a family station, is a huge place consisting of two lighthouse towers standing 333 feet apart, with two cottages and gardens at each tower, once the home of four families. The space between the two establishments is simply meadowland with a disused engine room (with huge fog trumpets on the roof) located roughly halfway between the two. The Low Light of the two was discontinued in about 1923 leaving the High Light as the sole navigation aid. The high tower stands 125 feet high.

Nash Point

Nash Point

In common with many other stations at which I had served, Nash had a First Order Fresnel lens, a precision-made piece of engineering incorporating a series of glass prisms that completely surrounded the light. Many of these were mounted in a trough of mercury and rotated to produce a flashing code. I was astonished to find that the engineers planned to remove the lens entirely and replace it with a

Disassembled lens panels

Top part of lens

modern piece of electrical equipment. Watching as the precision-made segments were carefully disassembled, piece by piece, was fascinating, as I had never seen this done before. Although in a way it was sad to see it happening, it was an operation worth witnessing. The removed lens was later reassembled on a lower floor of the tower to be used as a possible tourist attraction in the future.

It was with a great deal of sadness that after 32 years' service I finally left the Trinity House Lighthouse Service on 15 September 1998, a lifelong job that I had thoroughly enjoyed, and one I was sure I would miss.

The Royal Albert Hall

Within a month of taking up my retirement I received a call from Trinity House inviting me to the Albert Hall in November along with an ex-colleague, Phil Griffiths, and the Deputy Master of Trinity House, Admiral Rowe, to represent the Lighthouse Service at the Festival of Remembrance. The year 1998 was the first time that Trinity House had been represented at the festival, and I was absolutely delighted to be asked. The actual ceremony of remembrance was to take place on Saturday 7 November, but I was surprised to learn that for everything to go as well as seen on television there were to be several rehearsals for all involved. The Albert Hall is a very imposing circular red-brick building which stands directly opposite Kensington Gardens and the recently-renovated Albert Memorial, and it was here that our little group met with members of the civilian services who were taking part in the ceremony with us: police, specials, nurses, and Thames River Police, etc. Our instructor, and the man who for the previous 18 years had been in charge of organising the entrance of everyone into the arena on the night, was the ramrod straight, six-foot six-inch tall Garrison Sergeant Major Perry Mason. After taking us to a quiet staircase, he drilled us on how to march in step up and down a staircase. Upon entering the main hall we practised a dummy run

Royal Albert Hall

marching across the vast arena floor, climbing the raised stage directly opposite our proposed entrance, then up the steep bank of seating behind where the Band of Guards would sit on the night, to where we would ultimately end up as part of the initial muster. The huge amphitheatre with its strange mushroom-shaped acoustic dishes hanging from the domed ceiling echoed with the voices of other drill instructors putting their charges through their paces in an attempt to be perfect for the performance.

Although our time here was at a premium and it was a serious occasion, there were one or two lighter moments. On the Friday afternoon, standing not too far from us in our designated training area was a group of Chelsea Pensioners, not in their famous scarlet coats, but black. Our sergeant major, having just torn a strip off some TA boys, turned abruptly and was confronted by one of the pensioners just about to put a cigarette in his mouth. The sergeant didn't have to pull himself upright to his full height as he was already ramrod straight, but he bellowed in a low voice 'Take that thing out, it won't do you any good, it will make you sick', then after turning away he had second thoughts, spun on his heel, and bending forward from the waist and jutting out his chin he said to the pensioner 'and they KILL.' What a magical moment that was!

With the public admitted on Saturday afternoon, the matinee performance got underway, and we took our allotted places with the other groups assembling for the muster. Anxiously we waited for our turn to be called, and in the background we could faintly hear the band of Guards as the various groups made their entrance into the hall. We watched as the assembled gathering slowly grew smaller as each group ahead of us was ushered in at the precise time. Finally it was our turn and we found ourselves shuffling forward towards the curtained doorway where our Sergeant Major greeted us with reassurance, stood us in the correct position and whispered last minute instructions. Suddenly the curtains opened and we were hit by a bright spotlight, and the voice of Richard Baker was broadcasting to the nation (approximately six million) as well as to the gathered assembly. At the same time the Sergeant Major was giving us our pace instructions, 'Left, right, left, right ... stand by ... quick march', and while Richard Baker was finishing our introduction we started on our long descent, taking each step in time to the beat from a big drum as the band played us in. Then we were at the bottom of the steps and on the arena floor. While the Admiral, Phil and myself, picked out by spotlights in the darkness, marched across the floor to the applause of the audience, Richard Baker continued with the following introduction:

> Today we extend a special welcome and thanks to the last of our lighthouse keepers who are led by the Deputy Master of Trinity House, Rear Admiral Patrick Rowe. The Master of Trinity House, His Royal Highness The Duke of Edinburgh, will witness the closure of the last manned lighthouse in Britain at Broadstairs in Kent later this month. With lighthouses darkened during the Second World War, lighthouse men played a vital role for shipping marking safe lanes through the minefields to home ports with buoys. Gordon Medlicott and Phillip Griffiths have both been lighthouse keepers for over 30 years, but were made redundant when Nash Point Lighthouse in Wales was automated in August. Computers and modern technology mean that the lighthouse keeper is no more.

Having negotiated the vast arena floor we were seated directly behind the Band of Guards and were soon joined by the Chelsea Pensioners who received a standing ovation as well as the War Widows. It was while I was looking around this spectacular building that the thought struck me: this must be the biggest circular room that three Trinity House men have ever been in together. Despite the solemnity of the occasion, I was quite tickled by it!

The entertainment section of the festival was well-presented, with the armed forces showing precision drill work and disciplined marching routines, and the military bands played superbly to the joy of the audience. However, it was the prayers in the final section of the performance that were the most moving – a very emotional experience, especially when the bugle calls of the *Last Post* and *Sunset* are played. During the complete silence when the poppies fall from on high onto bowed heads is such a heart-rending time that there can't be a person in the hall that isn't affected.

In the evening, after the arrival of Her Majesty The Queen and Prince Philip, accompanied by Prince Andrew and Princess Anne, we did it all again. The performance was repeated in the same order as the matinee, but this time during our march across the floor we were told that Prince Philip, with a broad grin on his face, was seen to lean forward from the Royal Box to watch closely as 'his boys' performed!

To attend the festival was quite an experience and it is something I will remember for many years to come. I considered it a privilege, and felt proud to have been invited to represent the Lighthouse Service at such a time.

The last of the lighthouse keepers

My wife and I were soon to be guests of Trinity House once again, on this occasion it was to be at the final demanning ceremony of North Foreland on 26 November 1998. On the day, HRH The Prince Philip as Master and Rear Admiral Patrick Rowe, Deputy Master of Trinity House, accompanied by the Lord Lieutenant of the County and various Elder Brethren, greeted the last six keepers and then disappeared inside the lighthouse on a tour of inspection. HRH then mounted a rostrum outside the tower and delivered a speech declaring the automation of this lighthouse to be the culmination of 20 years' work and the end of a manned Lighthouse Service. I include here his full speech.

> Before I pull this string I would just like to say this is really quite an historic occasion today. It is the culmination of nearly 20 years' work to automate the lighthouses around the British Isles. Not done out of any malice, but simply because the technology is there and it's a more efficient way of doing it. I think there is a tendency to believe that automation means you can put in an automatic device and then forget all about the lighthouse, but that isn't what is going to happen. There will still be lighthouse attendants, and there will still be people monitoring and organising and managing the whole Lighthouse Service, so it's a stage in the development of the aids to navigation. But

of course change is one of those things which you always think is marvellous for other people, but it's never quite so pleasant when it's to do with yourself or other people for whom you're responsible. The lighthouse keepers of the Service have done a really tremendous job for over 400 years looking after the marks which are absolutely vital to the safety of ships and, in spite of the fact that there are radio and radar and GPS and everything else, it's still wonderfully comforting to actually see a light and know that that is where you are. And of course it's marvellous if for any reason your kit has broken down. So I would like to congratulate and to commiserate, I suppose, with the people who are leaving the Service, but I want to make it quite clear, that this is not the end of the Lighthouse Service, this is just one further development, and I hope this plaque here, this tablet, will remind people of the Service that has been rendered by lighthouse keepers and what a marvellous job they have done over so many years, and how their successors are going to go on ensuring that these vital aids to navigation are going to be maintained.

Following the speech Prince Philip came over to meet the invited guests and neighbours assembled under marquees on the lighthouse lawns; he even stopped and spoke to my wife and myself. With the departure of Prince Philip and the other dignitaries there was plenty of opportunity to look around the tower, which looked very different with the latest technology installed. I could recall some of the old equipment that I had operated through the years and had been responsible for – a very different day and age. So with the old cliché 'the end of an era' coming to mind, I was pleased that I had been there at the end to see the 'last' of the lighthouse keepers leave. I only hope that the trust placed in this new technology will prove to be founded.

Dinner with HRH The Prince Philip

Before the year was out I was especially surprised to learn that with the demanning of North Foreland, and the Lighthouse Service becoming completely automated, the Elder Brethren, in recognition of the loyal service given by keepers, had arranged for a Lighthouse Keepers' Service of Thanksgiving. This was to be held at St Olave's Church, London, followed by a farewell dinner at their headquarters, Trinity House on Tower Hill, in December 1998. His Royal Highness The

Duke of Edinburgh, as Master of Trinity House, would preside over the event. Invitations were sent to past keepers and their wives (or guest).

H.R.H. The Master and the Elder Brethren of

Trinity House
Request the company of

Mr and Mrs G. Medlicott

At the Lighthouse Keepers' Thanksgiving Service,
St Olave's Church, Hart Street, London EC3

On Tuesday 15th December 1998 at 6pm
And afterwards to Dinner at Trinity House

Dress: Lounge Suit   Carriages: 10.30.

Arrangements had been made for us to be picked up by coach from our hotel at Waterloo for transfer to St Olave's Church. With the theme of the evening to be associated with lighthouses we found the winding pathway from the gateway to the church door illuminated with open-flamed torches that flickered and sizzled in the rain, and the interior of the church lit only by small candles. The church is an ancient one, the first mention of it being made in 1109, and during the Great Fire in 1666 it was saved from destruction by the efforts of Samuel Pepys, the Master of Trinity House. Samuel and his wife were regular members of the congregation and are buried in the chapel. On display at the front of the church was a fine model of a tower rock lighthouse and a lightvessel.

With the arrival of HRH The Prince Philip the Service of Thanksgiving began, the maritime and light theme being continued throughout the service. On completion of the service, and after the departure of Prince Philip the congregation left the church to walk the short distance to the Trinity House building. Trinity House is the headquarters of the Lighthouse Service and is an elegant building of classical lines, which I believe is the equal of any of the other great buildings of London. Its interior, although a working office, is furnished with some impressive pictures and antiquities of nautical history that would not be out of place in a maritime museum. Over an imposing central staircase is a Gainsborough painting of immense proportions depicting the Court of Elder Brethren. Each guest was announced by name and presented to HRH The Prince Philip and Admiral Rowe, who were both formally dressed in long naval frock coats with rows of brass buttons, and then over drinks groups of ex-colleagues and old friends engaged in conversation. Dinner was announced, and was served in the magnificent library which was laid out with 12 circular tables, each table being named after a well-known lighthouse with a brightly-coloured lighthouse tower as a centrepiece. The top table was named Eddystone, its centrepiece being one of the much-admired Trinity House antiques in the form of a silver replica of Winstanley's 1698 Eddystone tower, a magnificently detailed object standing over 12 inches high. Having been pre-warned that my wife and I were to be seated at the top table, I had a feeling that the hand-crafted leather chair bearing a gilded crest at the head of the table wasn't mine, which the place name card confirmed.

The gathering fell silent as HRH entered the room and took his seat, my ex-colleague Mike O'Sullivan to the right, and I to his left. The seating then continued with my wife Louise, Admiral Rowe, Mrs Rowe, Sir Brian McGrath (Equerry), Gerry Douglas-Sherwood (my ex-colleague and opposite number with whom I worked on two stations over a period of seven years), and Mrs O'Sullivan completing the company. Conversation with Prince Philip was not as difficult as anticipated, and despite my earlier apprehension he was easy to talk to. We spoke of many things, mainly the job and things maritime of course, but also of grandchildren, something we had in common. He was a most pleasant and interesting man. At the end of the meal the toasts were made, HRH proposed 'The Queen', followed by Admiral Rowe who proposed 'The Queen Mother and Royal Family'. Prince Philip as Master then presented his speech, which thanked not only keepers for their devoted and loyal service, but also their wives and families who had given their support, which was recognised as an invaluable part of the Service. It was of course mentioned that it was sad to see the end of such an historical part of our maritime heritage. There then followed a toast by the Master and Elder Brethren to 'the keepers'. When HRH resumed his seat, the Deputy Master stood and presented his compliments, announcing that each of the keepers assembled was to be presented with a specially commissioned commemorative medal, and that the Elder Brethren from each table would make the presentation. The ladies were given a box of handmade chocolates emblazoned with the Trinity House coat of arms. My medal was presented to me by the Admiral, and on opening it, Prince Philip took it from its box to inspect it more closely, asking which lighthouse was depicted on it (Smeaton's Eddystone tower of 1759). The presentation, or the existence of the medal is probably the best-kept secret in the history of Trinity House as we had no inkling of it, but I was absolutely thrilled to receive it, a great treasure to pass on to my children and grandchildren.

Lighthouse keepers' medallion

Following the presentation Dermot Cronin, as senior Principal Keeper, responded to the toasts, making an excellent speech on our behalf, for which he received a well-deserved standing ovation. This drew the meal to an end, and Prince Philip bade us goodnight and left. The dinner was an unprecedented event, one into which a great deal of thought and planning had gone, and I can't think of anything that could have been done to make the evening more special. It was a tremendous way to end my service with Trinity House. I was later asked, and I agreed, to donate my service uniform for display at the South Stack Visitor's Centre based at that lighthouse, so my presence there will live on a little longer.

TRINTY HOUSE CAP BADGE

One of the oldest in existence, consisting of a replica of the Order of the Garter surrounding a lion rampant. The Order of the Garter was constituted by Edward III in 1348. The badge now consists of the Order of the Garter surrounding four ships of the Trinity House crest surmounted by a lion rampant.

No regrets

Looking back over my career with Trinity House I have few regrets. Although my children grew up without me and I was away from home at some critical and important stages of their lives, I did the job with their blessing, and for that I thank them.

Having been a seaman I knew the importance that ships' navigators placed on 'making' a light, so during the early days of operating oil lights I had a great deal of satisfaction in knowing that my light would have been a welcome sight to someone somewhere. I also knew that in fog ships slowed down, kept a radar watch and doubled the lookouts, and if close inshore listened for the sound of foghorns. Despite the hardships of firing an explosive signal I did feel that I had done a worthwhile job.

After retiring I became a volunteer and trained as an interpretation guide at one of the north-west's leading tourist attractions, Wigan Pier, a Victorian heritage centre depicting the social and local history of Wigan, my home town. I am often asked what my working background was before becoming a volunteer and, after the amazement of finding a lighthouse keeper in their midst, visitors often ask what it is I miss most.

Having been born and brought up near the sea, and having worked on it for most of my life, with six years in the Merchant Navy and 32 years in the Lighthouse Service, I suppose it is inevitable that what I miss is the sight, smell and sound of it. The sea and the marine environment hold a great fascination for many people, even those who have no connection to it, hence the numbers of people who flock to the beaches and small harbours at seaside resorts. It is difficult to say just what that fascination is, possibly the tranquillity of the water and the whole atmosphere generated in and around it. But the sea must be seen in its true context along with all the other activities associated with and surrounding it. Both its calmness and its turbulence have a great beauty that can only be appreciated by those who constantly live with it. However, the sea can never be taken for granted or treated with contempt, because it will always have the last word; it has become the final resting place of many a foolish person.

Throughout history the sea has bred a tightly-knit fellowship of those who have earned a living from it, and disregarding colour, creed or nationality, will risk life and limb to aid the other without hesitation or recompense. I consider myself lucky that throughout my working life I have been a part of that fellowship.

Appendices

Pharology – the science or study of
lighthouse design and engineering

Appendix I

DATA FOR THE LIGHTHOUSES I SERVED AT

Station name	Built	Height of tower in feet	Light above MHWS[1] in feet	Type of optical lens	Character[2]
Hartland Point	1874	60	120	Third Order bi-form 2 tiers	Gp Fl (6) W. 15s
Bull Point	1879	55	152	Third Order catadioptric	Gp Fl (3) W. 10s
Flatholm Island	1737	97	162	First Order catadioptric drum	R Gp Occ(2) W. 10s
Lundy North	1897	55	164	First Order	Gp Fl (2) W. 20s
Lynmouth Foreland	1900	50	220	First Order dioptric	Gp Fl (4) W. 15s
Strumble Head	1908	55	150	First Order catadioptric	Gp Fl (4) W. 15s
Lundy South	1897	50	175	Fourth Order catadioptric	Fl W. 5s
Portland Breakwater	1844	71	84	Fourth Order	Fl W. 10s
Point Robert, Sark	1913	30	110	Second Order catadioptric	Fl W. 15s
Quenard Point, Alderney	1912	106	112	First Order catadioptric	Gp Fl W. (4) 15s
Coquet Island	1723	72	81	First Order catadioptric	W. Occ
South Stack	1809	90	200	First Order catadioptric	Fl W. 10s
Bardsey Island	1821	99	130	First Order catadioptric	Gp Fl (5) W. 15s
St Bees Head	1718	55	336	First Order catadioptric	Gp Fl (2) W. 20s

Station name	Built	Height of tower in feet	Light above MHWS[1] in feet	Type of optical lens	Character[2]
Longstone	1826	88	75	Small Third Order twin catadioptric	Fl W. 20s
Inner Dowsing Tower	1971	212	142	Multicatadioptric ex-lightvessel	Fl W. 5s
Needles	1859	110	80	Second Order catadioptric drum	Gp Occ (2) W R G 20s
Flamborough Head	1806	89	214	First Order catadioptric	Gp Fl (4) W. 15s
North Foreland	1790	80	188	First Order catadioptric drum	Gp Fl (5) W.R. 20s
St Ann's Head	1714	32	147	First Order catadioptric drum	Fl W.R. 5s
Lizard Point	1751	62	230	Second Order catadioptric	Fl W.3s
Nash Point	1832	125	182	First Order drum	Gp Fl (2) W.R.
Bar Light Float			65		Fl W. 5s
Trwyn-Du	1838	96	61	First Order catadioptric	Fl (1) W. 5s
Point Lynas	1834	37	128	Second Order catadioptric drum	W. Occ 10s
Skerries	1714	75	120	First Order catadioptric	Gp. Fl (2) W. 10s
St Tudwal's	1877	20	151	Second Order catadioptric drum	Fl (1) W. 20s
Mumbles	1794	55	125	Sealed beam unit	Gp Fl (4) W. 10s

1   MHWS   Mean High Water Springs, which indicates the average height of the tides following a full moon when the tidal range is more extreme, with higher and lower tides than normal.

2   Each lighthouse is identified by its own flashing code, known officially as its 'character'. The number of flashes within a given time, e.g. one flash every five seconds, or two flashes every ten seconds (more than one flash in quick succession is deemed a group). The entry in the Admiralty List of Lights publication would appear as: Gp Fl (2) W 20s indicating that the light gives two quick white flashes followed by darkness, repeated every 20 seconds.

Appendix 2

HORNSBY OIL ENGINE

Painted dark green and surrounded by a polished (and totally inadequate) guard rail, the most prominent feature of this engine was its six foot diameter flywheel and huge horizontal shafts. A compressor attached to one side of the engine provided the required air pressure to operate the fog signal; valve wheels situated at head height at various intervals along the oversized pipework were the size of dinner plates. The air was pumped into three large storage tanks to a pressure of 125 psi, and the timing of the signal was done by a clockwork actuating clock mounted on a nearby wall, its long pendulum rotating a cam wheel that would

open an actuating valve at the correct time. To maintain the signal the clockwork had to be wound every hour by means of an endless chain that ran over a cog wheel moulded to take the links of the chain.

To start the engine it was first necessary to heat the cylinder head. This was achieved with a large floor-mounted blowlamp situated beneath a 'hot bulb' head at the end of the single cylinder. After 10–15 minutes a squirt of fuel was injected into the hot bulb, followed by an injection of compressed air, which would cause an explosion when mixed with the hot fuel vapour that was strong enough to drive the huge piston and flywheel forward. After the initial kick it was necessary to inject further shots of air into the cylinder on each compression stroke to maintain the impetus until the engine reached a speed where it could sustain itself. Once the engine was running it was a dream, the big single piston shunting backwards and forwards, and the flywheel running at about 90 rpm was surprisingly quiet, and was a real delight.

Appendix 3

Explosive fog signal

Hands-on experience in handling explosives during basic training would have been the ideal, but knowledge of the procedure was instead gained by word of mouth from colleagues at the lighthouses where they were used. The following instructions, drawn from experience, describe a procedure that is safe and effective.

Instructions for use

- The firing jib is operated up and down over the lantern roof by means of a handle, usually situated inside the lantern. Contact for firing is made by one electrical contact on the jib meeting another on the roof, thereby completing a circuit from the detonator to the exploder.
- Always keep the contacts clean and the worm gear and disc wheel well greased.
- Always fire away from the wind.
- Take a single detonator and insert it into the explosive charge, wrap the connecting wires around the body of the charge in a half-hitch, so that when connected to the tumbler the charge hangs upside down.
- First keep the switch on the firing panel in the neutral position; lower the jib into the loading position and squeeze together the two ends of the spring clip at the tumbler so that the holes correspond, insert one wire of the detonator into each of the clips ensuring that the bare ends (not the insulating sheath) make contact.
- Wind the jib arm to its full extent, and ensure the charges are hanging down and not thrown over the jib arm.

- Wind and set the graduated signal clock which will strike at the required time, select firing position 1 or 2 on the control panel, raise the plunger on the exploder box and fire on the bell.
- Have a tumbler (complete with clips) handy, and check at intervals that the clips on the jib are not damaged as these are occasionally blown off by the explosion.

Explosive fog signal in action at Coquet Lighthouse

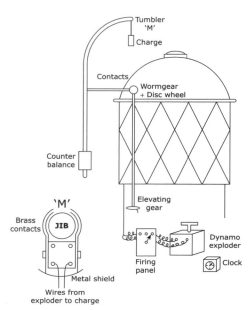

Diagram of fog signal

Appendix 4

INCANDESCENT OIL BURNER (IOB)

Oil under pressure flowing into a pre-heated vaporising tube forms a gas which issues from a nipple. As it travels up into the burner head, it strikes a deflector cone where part of it is diverted back through two gasways to Bunsen tubes placed each side of the vaporising tube. The remainder of the gas passes upwards into the head where it is lit to illuminate an incandescent mantle.

After pre-heating, the lamp becomes self-sustaining by means of the diverted gas remaining alight at the Bunsen tubes, thereby providing a constant supply of vapour gas.

In 1901, retired gas engineer Arthur Kitson invented a new type of burner in which, instead of the oil being vaporised at the wick and burning as an open flame, as in the standard Argand and Douglass lamps in use at that time, the oil was vaporised and mixed with air in a container under pressure to form an inflammable gas that could be burned in an incandescent mantle.

In 1922 David Hood, Engineer-in-Chief to Trinity House, improved the lamp, making it simpler to operate. It used less fuel, and gave a brighter light. This lamp then became the standard form of illumination for lighthouses until 1975.

Incandescent mantle

The mantle is made of a textile fabric impregnated with thorium and ceramic, which leaves a shell of thorium oxide when burned.

Coupled with the Chance Bros' optical lens, the paraffin vapour lamp was capable of producing a light of 1,000,000 candle power.

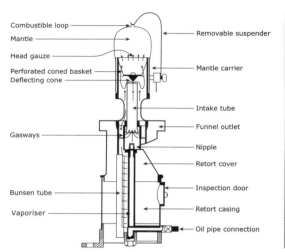

Combustible loop

Mantle

Head gauze

Perforated coned basket
Deflecting cone

Gasways

Bunsen tube

Vaporiser

Removable suspender

Mantle carrier

Intake tube

Funnel outlet

Nipple

Retort cover

Inspection door

Retort casing

Oil pipe connection

Hood incandescent oil burner

Appendix 5

KEEPERS' PAY SCALE 1968

With effect from 2 July 1968 the following pay scale
will apply to permanent keepers

Rates of Pay

Supernumerary Assistant Keepers	£627 per annum for the first three months. £702 per annum fixed thereafter. This rate will be paid until appointed Assistant Keeper.
Assistant Keepers	£745 per annum on appointment, thence by annual increments of £6 to £781 per annum with a further three increments of £10 each on the completion of 9–12 and 15 years' service in the grade to a maximum of £811.
Principal Keepers	£880 per annum on appointment, thence by annual increments of £10 to a maximum of £930 per annum.

Supernumerary Assistant Keepers, if not appointed as Assistant Keeper before the completion of five years' service, are to be appointed to that grade irrespective of whether there are vacancies and are to receive all the emoluments of Assistant Keepers including house allowance.

On appointment to Assistant Keeper, SAKs are to enter at the minimum of the Assistant Keeper's Scale, *viz*: £745 per annum, whether or not they have completed five years' service as Supernumerary Assistant Keeper.

Allowances

House	Principal and Assistant Keepers; 9s.0d. per diem w.e.f. 1.1.67. Payable continuously to keepers at all lighthouses where quarters are not provided. (At certain land lighthouses where quarters are available but not on the normal scale an allowance of 4s. 0d. per diem is paid to the second Assistant Keeper).
Quarters and additional quarters	Supernumerary Assistant Keepers only: 4s.0d. per diem w.e.f. 1.1.67. Payable at all times when quarters are not provided. An additional quarters allowance of 5s. 0d. per diem is paid continuously to all married Supernumerary Assistant Keepers.
Victualling	All keepers: 6s. 0d. per diem w.e.f. 1.5.68. Payable while on duty at all rock lighthouses including travelling time to and from them.
Rock	All keepers: 2s. 6d. per diem payable in respect of each day or part of a day on duty at the following Lighthouses: Longstone, Coquet, Casquets, Alderney, Eddystone, Longships, Wolf Rock, Round Island, Bishop Rock, Nab Tower, Lundy North, Lundy South, Flatholm, Smalls, South Bishop, Skokholm, Bardsey Island, Skerries.
Consolidated daily rate on a station basis in respect of the following allowances as appropriate[1]	Fog machinery allowance Fog sounding allowance Electric allowance Radio telephone allowance Radio beacon allowance Calibration beacon allowance Garden allowance
Substitution pay	The senior Assistant Keeper when in charge of a lighthouse during the absence of the Principal Keeper is to receive the minimum of the scale of pay of Principal Keepers and also the appropriate allowances in lieu of his own pay and allowances.

Off station	Principal and Assistant Keepers 6s. 0d. per diem w.e.f. 1.5.68. payable if required to carry out duty at a Land Lighthouse other than that to which they have been appointed or at which they have their houses.
Travelling	Thames River lights attendant only £120 per annum.
Special	Thames River attendant only £25 per annum.
Scilly Isles Condition	Bishop Rock and Round Island Lighthouses. Principal and Assistant Keepers who reside with their families in the Scilly Isles: 8s. 6d. per week w.e.f. 1.2.67.
Annual Leave on Pay and Free From Duty Periods On Pay	(a) Principal Keepers and Assistant Keepers at Shore Lighthouses are allowed 28 days' annual leave except at the following lighthouses when the annual leave is 35 days. Start Point, Trevose, Bull Point, Nash, St Ann's, Souter, Whitby and Flamborough. (b) Supernumerary Assistant Keepers 17 days increasing to 28 days after four years' service. (c) No annual leave is granted to Principal Keepers and Assistant Keepers stationed at rock lighthouses in view of their four weeks' free from duty period ashore following each period of eight weeks' duty at the lighthouse. (d) Supernumerary Assistant Keepers are allowed free from duty periods ashore at the rate of one week for every month spent at a rock lighthouse.

1   The consolidated daily allowance rates to be paid at the various stations are given on page 125.

Notes

Uniform clothing is supplied.

A life assurance policy (annual premium £3 paid by Trinity House) is effected after one year's service.

Free removal of furniture on transfer is not allowed until completion of five years' service as Supernumerary Assistant Keeper or until appointed Assistant Keeper, whichever is earlier.

TRINITY HOUSE
LONDON, E.C.3.

November 1968

Pay scale (1968)

The following table details the consolidated daily rate in respect of the following allowances at each lighthouse:

Fog signal machinery
Fog sounding
Electric
Radio beacon
Calibration beacon
Radio telephone
Garden

The set allowance was paid irrespective of whether the lighthouse operated one or a number of the services listed. Therefore, a keeper at Cromer would be paid a single payment of 9d. even if that station had a fog signal, a radio beacon and electric equipment.

	Principal Keeper	Assistant Keeper
Cromer	9d.	7d.
Lowestoft	5d.	–
Withernsea	9d.	–
North Foreland	7d.	5d.
Dungeness	1s. 4d.	1s. 1d.
St Catherines	1s. 0d.	9d.
Anvil Point	5d.	4d.
Beachy Head	1d.	1d.
Nab Tower	2s. 4d.	1s. 5d.
Needles	1s. 6d.	9d.
Portland Bill	8d.	6d.
Alderney	4d.	3d.
Casquets	2/-	1s. 1d.
Hanois	1s. 8d.	10d.
Sark	4d.	3d.
Bishop Rock	5d.	4d.
Eddystone	2s. 2d.	1s. 2d.
Lizard	1s. 1d.	10d.
Longships	5d.	4d.

	Principal Keeper	Assistant Keeper
Pendeen	10d.	8d.
Penlee Point	5d.	4d.
Round Island	2s. 3d.	1s. 3d.
St Anthony	6d.	3d.
Start Point	1s. 2d	11d.
Trevose Head	4d.	3d.
Wolf Rock	1s. 8d.	10d.
Bull Point	7d.	5d.
Flatholm	9d.	7d.
Hartland	1s. 4d.	7d.
Lundy North	1s. 2d.	10d.
Lundy South	1s. 4d.	7d.
Lynmouth Fore	4d.	3d.
Nash Point	4d.	3d.
St Ann's	1s. 0d.	10d.
Strumble head	4d.	3d.
Bardsey Island	1s. 9d.	11d.
Coquet Island	6d.	5d.
Flamborough	1s. 1d.	10d.
Longstone	2s. 2d.	1s. 3d.
St Bees Head	5d.	4d.
St Marys	2d.	2d.
Skerries	2s. 1d.	1s. 2d.
Skokholm	1s. 9d.	11d.
Smalls	5d.	4d.
Souter Point	1s. 1d.	10½d.
South Bishop	2s. 1d.	2s. 1d.
South Stack	1s. 5d.	8d.
Whitby	9d.	8d.

Note

All Supernumerary Assistant Keepers are to be paid the appropriate consolidated daily rate for Assistant Keepers for the period they are on the station concerned.

Appendix 6

Global Positioning System (GPS)

The Global Positioning System that is today used throughout the world for accurate position fixing and navigation was designed and is maintained by the US Military for use in the guidance of missiles. Despite its origins and intent GPS is available to everyone who owns a moderately-priced receiver. It is installed in many new cars for in-car navigation and is also used by the principal airlines and shipping companies, by ramblers, canoeists, yachtsmen, police, ambulances, fire engines, utility companies and rescue services, as well as the military.

At its inception, to prevent misuse of the system by hostile powers, the US encrypted some of the information, thereby deliberately downgrading it to provide an accuracy of only 100 metres. Since other safeguards are now in place to ensure the integrity of the US defence system, the everyday use of GPS is good for an accuracy of 10 metres.

Information for position-fixing is provided by a series of 24 satellites circling the earth, and it is only necessary to obtain information from three of these to be able to fix a position. A service now offered is DGPS, that is GPS with corrections, that offers accurate positioning to within 2–3 metres. Trinity House provides this service free of charge, the signal bearing the corrected information being transmitted by a second carrier on radio beacon frequencies from six lighthouses.

Flamborough Head
North Foreland
St Catherines
Lizard
Nash Point
Point Lynas

Appendix 7

THE MEN I WORKED WITH AT EACH STATION

PK = Principal Keeper   SAK = Supernumerary Assistant Keeper
TPK = Temporary Principal Keeper   AK = Assistant Keeper

Hartland Point
Peter Edwards PK
Ron Smith PK
Brian Stock SAK
Richard Lambert SAK
Gareth Attley SAK
Ivor Pritchard AK
Ron Churchill AK
Tony Homewood AK

Bull Point
Bill Mortimer PK
Kevin Wood AK
Roy Howes AK
Cliff Bell AK

Flatholm
Colin Nicholls PK
Eddie Bell AK
Dave Erickson AK
Bob Kett AK

Lundy North
Fred Jones PK
Brian Twigg SAK
Neil Hammond AK
Ted Townsend AK

Lynmouth Foreland	Frank Harris PK
	Alan Callaghan AK
Strumble Head	Terry Creswell AK
	Alan Wilson AK
Lundy South	Arthur Robertson PK
	Bob Collis PK
	Cyril Jones PK
	Jim Thompson AK
	Chris Tye AK
	Bob Farrah AK
	Les McSalley AK
Portland Breakwater	Harry Fenn PK
	Simon Reynolds AK
	J. Cameron AK
Sark	Norman Wakely PK
	Ian Patterson AK
	Bill Humphries AK
	John Corrie AK
	Andy Middlemiss AK
	Peter Hoctor AK
Alderney	Eric Dove PK
	C. Jacques SAK
	Mike Hardy SAK
	Brian Bayliss AK
	Peter Lee AK
	Fred Sherlock AK
Coquet	Fred Jones PK
	G. Peacock PK
	Gerry McKenna SAK
	Jack Hodkinson AK
	Bill Bolton AK
	Paul Brodiak AK
	David Vyse AK

South Stack	Mac Macpherson PK
	Stan Booth PK
	John Nelson SAK
	Kelvin Keeble SAK
	Mark Hunter AK
	Barry Cooke AK
	Norman Grindle AK
	Dermot Cronin AK
	Bob Kett AK
	Gordon Phillips AK
Bardsey	Peter Riches AK
	Richard Vose AK
St Bees	Osie Murphy PK
Longstone	Mac Macpherson PK
	Ken Rowley PK
	John Graham AK
	John Cooney AK
	John Turney AK
	Paul Brodiak AK
	Mark Shipley AK
	Ian McKintyre AK
Inner Dowsing	Barry Lingwood AK
	John Mobbs AK
	Ian Cairns AK
Needles	Phil Griffiths PK
	Paul Davies AK
	Gerry Douglas-Sherwood AK
	Tony Elvers AK
	Larry Walker AK
	Frank Creasey AK
	Peter Halil AK
	Dave Knight AK
	John Nelson AK
	Tim Surplice AK
	Peter Robson AK
	Mark Shipley AK
	Ian McIntyre AK

Holyhead Control	Bill O'Brien PK
	Peter Riches AK
	Peter Halil AK
	Gerry McKenna AK
	Steve Davies AK
	Les McSalley AK
	Chris Foulds AK
	Colin Brown Labourer/driver
North Foreland	Gerry Douglas-Sherwood TPK
	Peter Robson AK
	Tony Dawson AK
	Bill Scott AK
	Denis Flintstone AK
	Chris Foulds AK
	Brian Clayton AK
	Les McSalley AK
	Barry Simmonds AK
	Paul Jellis AK
Flamborough	Frank Wilson PK
	Bob Wilkinson AK
Lizard	Eddie Matthews PK
	John Turney AK
	Frank Creasey AK
Nash Point	Colin Bales AK
	Barry Simmonds AK
	Chris Foulds AK

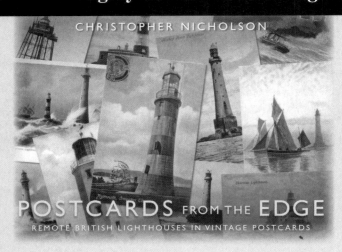

- Snapshots from the past of Britain's remotest lighthouses

- Complemented with a host of historical facts tracing the historical importance of the ubiquitous postcard

We've been sending one another postcards for well over a century now — usually brief messages to our friends and family telling them about the weather on our holidays or where we're visiting next on our travels.

A hundred years ago we sent postcards with more serious messages — important, personal information about births, marriages and deaths, urgent requests for help, or just to keep in touch before the use of the telephone became widespread.

The choice of subjects featured on postcards is vast, but amongst the most popular has always been the lighthouse — a symbol of safety and reliability, and evidence of Man's basic instinct to warn and reassure. Over the years, almost every British lighthouse has featured on a postcard of some description.

This new book from Christopher Nicholson, author of the highly-acclaimed *Rock Lighthouses of Britain*, concentrates on vintage postcards featuring the remotest lighthouses of all. Within these pages are snapshots of the past from the very edge of Britain — granite pillars rising from sea-swept reefs or the lights on uninhabited storm-lashed islets dotted around the coasts of England, Wales and Scotland.

Some of these cards are artists' impressions, some are hand-tinted, while others are real sepia or black and white photographs — but they all show how things used to look and how life used to be at the very extremes of offshore Britain. Due to their age these postcards are now valuable documents of social history — keepers posing with their families or being relieved at the end of their stint of duty — and they also illustrate the changing appearance of the lighthouses, together with the appalling weather the keepers endured. Proof, if such were needed, that there was nowhere too isolated nor weather too rough that would daunt the determined postcard photographer!

It was perhaps because of the very remoteness of the lighthouses that drew people to buy the postcards and these evocative photographs will invoke an appreciation of those bygone times. With chapters on 'pillar lights', 'island lights', 'relief days', 'wild winds and white water' and 'curiosities' the author has been given unique access to the collections of private individuals and lighthouse authorities to compile a fascinating and nostalgic work. Each lighthouse featured is accompanied by interesting historical details as well as a selection of vintage postcard views with extended captions — some over a century old.

liberally illustrated   colour throughout   softback   December 2009

from **Whittles Publishing**, Dunbeath, Caithness, Scotland. KW6 6EY, UK
Tel: +44(0)1593-731 333; Fax: +44(0)1593-731 400;
e-mail: info@whittlespublishing.com • www.whittlespublishing.com